for Denver Phil
for Tina & Jack Simon

Published in 2014 by Kyle Books
www.kylebooks.com
general.enquiries@kylebooks.com
www.kylebooks.com

Distributed by National Book Network
4501 Forbes Blvd., Suite 200
Lanham, MD 20706
Phone: (800) 462-6420
Fax: (800) 338-4550
customercare@nbnbooks.com

First published in Great Britain in 2013 by
Kyle Books, an imprint of Kyle Cathie Ltd.

10 9 8 7 6 5 4 3 2 1

ISBN 978-1-909487-14-7

Editor **Judith Hannam**
Editorial Assistant **Tara O'Sullivan**
Copy Editor **Jo Richardson**
Designer **Helen Bratby**
Photographer **Peter Cassidy**
Illustrator **K-Fai Steele**
Food Stylist **Mima Sinclair**
Prop Stylist **Iris Bromet**
Production **Nic Jones and David Hearn**

Library of Congress Control
Number: 2014937478

Color reproduction by ALTA London
Printed and bound in China by Toppan
Leefung Printing Ltd

Important note The information contained
in this book is intended as a general guide
to curing and smoking and is based on the
authors' own experimentation, experience,
and research. Neither the authors nor the
publishers can be held responsible for the
consequences of the application or
misapplication of any of the information
or ideas presented in this book.

PORK

Preparing, curing & cooking all that's possible from a pig

BY PHIL VICKERY & SIMON BODDY
PHOTOGRAPHY PETER CASSIDY

KYLE BOOKS

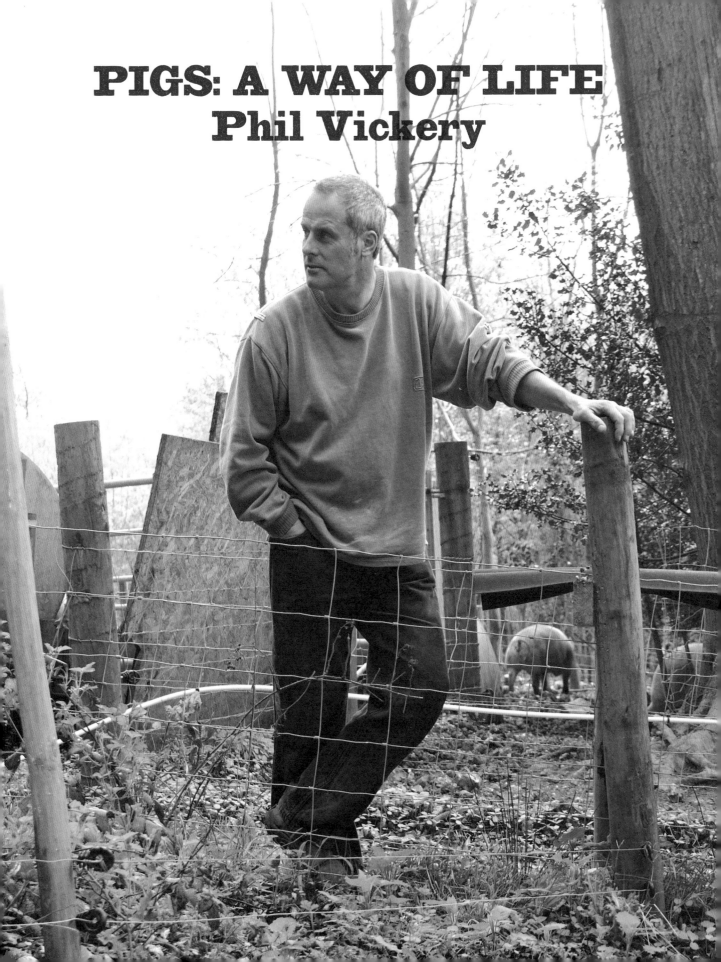

PIGS: A WAY OF LIFE
Phil Vickery

y fascination with pigs started at an early age. I vividly remember my father buying half a pig from a local farmer and cutting it up at home to pop into the freezer for the winter months. We lived in the country. I'm sure this was not an everyday occurrence, but it seemed quite normal to us. It was the first time I had seen a dead animal ever, let alone in the house. My father would not only cut and tie the whole thing up but also use all the extremities. Even to this day, like my brothers and me, he adores trotters and always asks me to get him a couple when I go to the butcher shop. Another of his great favorites was brawn. I can still see it now, a quivering jellified mold of chunks of pig head, tongue, and brain. He would make it in a Pyrex bowl and turn it onto a white enamel plate with a dark blue edge. That was our afternoon snack, along with bread and sometimes piccalilli.

The first book I ever read on cooking was given to me by the local church caretaker. I must have been eight or nine, and, according to my mother, had never shown any real interest in cooking before, so I'm not quite sure why he gave it to me. I think he was trying to keep me occupied while my father helped to clean up after an event. The book was the 1936 edition of *Warne's Everyday Cookery*, and it really fired me up with its wonderful color and black and white plates of elaborate dishes and preparation methods from chefs. Flipping through it some 40 or more years later, there in the front I found a recipe for my dad's brawn, written down by me, along with another of his favorites, bread pudding.

The farmer who supplied my dad was a lovely man named George King. He was a big man, soft spoken and always wearing a flat hat. His son Andrew helped him out on the farm and his mother ran the small store. My older brother Chris worked on the farm on Saturdays, helping out with various jobs, and one late-summer day he asked me if I would like to help spud picking. This entailed walking up and down the field picking up potatoes that had been spun out of the dry ground by the tractor. It was hard, back-breaking work, but I did enjoy it. Afterward, we would get a 56lb sack with a few bags of fruit thrown in and a small bottle of milk straight from the cow for our cornflakes.

I progressed from spud picking to feeding and watering the pigs. It took a good hour and involved jumping in and out of a long row of pigsties. George named each sty, and the first one I remember was called Barrel's, then Green Doors, The Piggery, and finally Kathmandu on the end, as it was the furthest away. We would grind the barley or wheat for feeding the pigs in a large mill with a huge hopper, then mix it with a pre-bought feed. On some Saturdays, a large van would appear carrying 20 or so flour bags crammed full of old bread, cakes, buns, and doughnuts from a local baker. Some were still good to eat and Andrew and I would stuff ourselves. The pigs, needless to say, would gorge themselves too. They also had great names such as Gertrude, a lovely Saddleback, and Queenie, a Duroc cross. Albert the boar would make sure they were all kept happy. Occasionally you would get a runt or a pig that wasn't quite right; Wibbly and Ted were classic examples. Wibbly walked sideways and had a constant shake, probably due to brain damage caused by her mother laying on her, but she was lovely, affectionate, and such a character. Ted was a boar runt with a large belly that almost dragged on the ground and a constant sniffle. Wibbly and Ted became good friends and lived in the barn, from where they would roam the farm. Both, I have to say, made great pork, probably because they really were free-range.

Those were good times—no *E. coli*, no restrictions on feed, no hassle, and above all great-tasting pork. This was small-scale production and way before I had even heard of intensive farming. I'm sure it existed, but the focus then was not on feeding regimes and state-of-the-art quick-growing feed but on well-reared, good-quality, delicious meat. In fact, all the hotels and restaurants I ever worked in always had a "pig man," who once a week would take away large bins filled with the leftover food. From there it was boiled, strained, cooled, and fed to pigs. That has all stopped due to very strict regulation. My belief is that we should return to those days because thousands of tons of perfectly good food are now being dumped into landfills. A lot of commercial pig food is bulked out with cooked, dry bakery products like George used to use, so to me there is no difference between that and "waste" food. But for this to work of course, the collection, cooking, and use of the food must be properly regulated and controlled, ensuring no raw meat or fish products are allowed to enter the food chain.

One thing I did learn with George was the cycle of pig rearing. Piglets were born, weaned, fed and fattened, and then sold. It was not by any means a large-scale operation, but it taught me that well-reared, well-looked-after, and well-fed pigs produce great-tasting end products. If you are about to embark on pig keeping or production, you have to be committed, in my eyes, to humane ways of rearing and housing, fresh water and good feed, and a peaceful existence. You also have to follow the process right through from cute piglets to the slaughterhouse. Yes, the final stage is unpleasant, but only then can you fully understand the importance of the whole cycle.

Slaughtering is not a pleasant experience, as I have said, but all the slaughterhouses I have been to treat the animals with great care and attention. A stressed animal is no good to anyone; adrenalin can cause havoc in fresh meat if the animal is not properly looked after. Simon, my butcher and co-author of this book, once called me to say that a pig carcass was like jelly due to adrenalin. I would much rather eat meat that I know has been reared and treated correctly and humanely from start to finish. I have, over the years, dabbled in pork production and gone to great lengths to ensure that all my animals had a good life.

I often get asked about rare and old pig breeds, and which offer the best and highest meat yield, lowest fat content, and so on. To me, there were and still are some fabulous breeds around. However, one of the main reasons some are no longer with us is because they either have a very low meat yield or are too fatty. I personally like Hampshire, Berkshire, and a cross between American Landrance, Duroc, and Chester White. Spotted pig is widely used these days by chefs, but it really depends on what you are going to do with the end product. The issue of pork's fat content always rears its head though, and the press is full of horror stories of this most demonized of food products. Some research even suggests that pork fat can actually be good for you in certain circumstances, and lean pork has less fat per pound than cottage cheese. The supermarkets have to take a little of the blame here. They say that their customers want a very small amount of fat on their meat, whereas those I talk to want more fat—not a lot, but slightly more. So I think it has a lot to do with a quicker turnaround of product; the longer you leave pigs to fatten, the more they cost you in feed.

From a chef's point of view, pork is an incredibly versatile meat. I always say that you can pretty much marry any flavor profile to it. Spices work well with pork; take for instance a pork vindaloo where the meat melds with the spicy fragrance and doesn't overpower the final dish. Sweet fruits such as mango, roasted pears, and raspberries are perfect, but equally sharp fruits such as rhubarb and lime or lemon also seem to go naturally with it. Some fish works well with pork too; lobster, shrimp, scallops, and even salmon make ideal partners. Cream, mustard, vinegars, oils, and many herbs are all fine with pork—it's truly fail-safe.

Many years ago, all over the world, many families kept a pig that was fattened for the lean winter months. The pig spent spring and summer gorging itself and when the time came provided the family with much-needed, highly nutritious food. Every part of the animal was prepared and eaten fresh or preserved. Salting and drying was the most popular preserving method. Preserving it in its own fat, or confit, is still practiced today by many chefs and restaurants, as it results in a very long shelf life.

Europe produces a dazzling array of preserved meats and it was on a filming trip in the south of Spain that I realized how much further we could take pig-rearing and production. I flew to Seville and then drove up to Aracena in the western Andalucian countryside to meet Miguel. He was responsible for overseeing the PR that surrounds arguably the world's best air-dried ham, jamón Ibérico. We toured the area—incredibly, the size of Holland—that produces these wonderful, happy, and, yes, tasty pigs. They feast on acorns and put on roughly a third of their weight in just three months. They are amazingly clever, deftly removing the outside husk of the acorn before eating the center and spitting out the rest. At about one year old they are rounded up and processed, packed in salt, and then left to hang for many months until the ham has produced a fantastic unrivaled sweetness. Some hams are eaten after only a few months but others are hung for as long as five years, all controlled by human eye, feel, and expertise. On saying goodbye to Miguel, we shook hands and he said "Trouble is Phil, you can't do this back home." On the plane I fell asleep but after a few minutes woke up and thought about what Miguel had said to me. Why can't we? We have pigs, we have salt, and we can mimic the temperature and, more importantly, the humidity.

So about ten years ago I bought some land and practiced producing ham, buying what I thought were the right breed and rearing them. What a disaster—moldy meat, tough, too dry, awful. I tried again, and failed again. I remember going to the slaughterhouse and the farmers slow hand clapping me as I tried to reverse a trailer. A good friend of mine, Peter Gott, once said to me, "Show me your hands." I did and he said, "You're not a real farmer, you haven't got enough s**t on your hands." Of course he was right, but he did agree to help me. I was about to give up when I was introduced to Simon Boddy, a big, gruff butcher with a disdain for chefs; I can't put in print what he called them. He didn't trust me and made that very clear. It turned out he was a master in curing and preserving. We became good friends and partners, and I found somebody that shared my passion for pigs and cured meats. His knowledge and experience is second to none, and his dedication to his work borders on obsession. We still joke with each other about those early days. When I decided to write a book on pork, I simply had to have Simon on board to help me. So here is the product of probably 60 years' sheer hard work and dedication. Yes, Miguel was right to a certain extent, but watch out, we're catching up!

PORK: A WAY OF LIFE
Simon Boddy

us scrofa domesticus, more commonly known as the domestic pig, has always been considered to be a subspecies of the wild boar. There is archaeological evidence, found in the Tigris basin in eastern Turkey, to suggest that the pig was domesticated from the wild boar as early as 13,000–12,700 BC, a process achieved by our ancestors with relative ease due to the adaptable and omnivorous nature of the creature. Wild boar were indigenous to Western Europe, including Great Britain, and were widespread by the Middle Ages. There is some debate as to whether wild boar populations were locally domesticated or the modern European domestic pig was produced by crossing native wild boars with domesticated Asian pigs. Pigs were first introduced to the US in the sixteenth century, brought over from Cuba. In the late 18th century, Chinese pigs were brought to the UK, and in 1830 a gray-black boar and sow were imported from Italy by a Lord Weston. These and other foreign breeds were introduced to improve the variety, quality, and quantity of the meat. Although there is not much authentic information available to explain how our breeds developed, I suspect that the breeds we know today owe a fair amount to this ancestry.

Although I have worked with pork for nearly 30 years, my real fascination began about 15 years ago. I had just lost a big customer and was looking for ways to replace the turnover. The pork industry in the UK at that time was on its knees and it was really tough for pig farmers. It was suggested to me that we could perhaps offer a service to farmers that would increase the value of their pigs, namely turning them into cured products such as bacon and sausages. I contacted *Farmers Weekly* and they ran an article on it. We started to get inquiries fairly quickly, and before long we began to process some pigs. I have to say that the venture exceeded my expectations and with the advent of farmers' markets in the late 1990s, it turned into a whole new career. Along with the extra business I started to learn about the various pig breeds and how different they all are.

By far the most popular pig breeds are what we generically call the heritage breeds, which include the Gloucestershire Old Spot, Tamworth, Large Black, Red Wattle, and the Saddleback. Unfortunately, I have no special affection for any of these breeds. There is a massive misconception that heritage breeds provide the most flavorful pork and the tastiest bacon and sausages, which is frankly an absolute load of crap. The reason these breeds are rare is because from a commercial point of view nobody wants them, and certainly not me! I mention the word "commercial" because the bulk of pork is produced commercially and you will hear no mention of a heritage breed on a commercial pig unit—but the term you will hear is "hybrid."

With pressure from consumers to have less fat and more meat, and pressure all around to have cheaper pork, we have over the years seen pig-improvement companies evolve and develop hybrid strains of pig to satisfy such demands. These companies will take certain breeds of pig and, using applied pig genetic development techniques, produce strains of breeding stock that fulfill the most stringent of requirements, i.e. a pig with a long lean back and double-muscled hams.

When I met Phil, the first pigs we processed together were Sandy and Black crosses. The estimated usable lean meat of these pigs was somewhere between 30 and 40 percent, which is simply not good enough for what we wanted to achieve. Don't get me wrong, the meat we did get was fantastic, but there was just not enough of it. I introduced Phil to a customer of mine who happened to be a pig farmer producing outdoor-reared weaners for one of the leading supermarkets. These pigs were a hybrid specifically bred to produce lean, well-muscled carcasses and could be kept on a free-range system. The biggest proportion of the breeding came from the Large White and Landrace, with Duroc and Hampshire providing the hardiness and intramuscular marbling, and Pietrain the muscle conformation. Our first batch of hybrid pigs went into some fenced-off woodland that we had access to and they were allowed to act like pigs should act—foraging and uprooting everything in their path—as well as being fed a feed ration with all the components in it to keep them healthy and fatten them for slaughter. They were nine months old at slaughter and as carcasses were just what we wanted to produce some wonderful charcuterie. After that, there was no looking back!

CHAPTER 1 Shoulder & ribs

The front end of any animal, especially the shoulder, often gets a bit forgotten. Yes, it's the fattiest part and when you balance out the meat to fat ratio it is far higher than, say, the loin or even ham. This, though, can be an advantage. A rolled pork shoulder or pork butt, for instance, will be delicious, even if slightly overdone, because the amount of fat they contain means they are constantly basted throughout the duration of cooking. The meat from the shoulder is also great for roasting, braising, or stewing, plus it makes excellent burgers. A pork burger can be very dry, but one using ground shoulder will be deliciously succulent because it's roughly 15–20 percent fat.

Simon always says that good salami is best made from carefully butchered meat from the shoulder. When we make salami together he "seams out" all the individual muscles (cuts where they are attached to each other or to the bone) and then mixes them with a proportion of good-quality fat. Sausages taste good primarily because the meat has a good fat content; remove that and the meat tastes dull. A lot of the sausages you can buy are made using any old scraps left over, but we take great care to get the right balance of good-quality meat, fat content, and seasoning.

Ribs have become extremely trendy over the past few years. Almost every café/brasserie/diner serves them in some way, shape, or form, which is not surprising as there is something enormously satisfying about diving into a rack of glistening, full-flavored, sticky ribs—real finger food! I was lucky enough to spend some time in North Carolina learning how to prepare and smoke them properly. The most important rule to remember is to cook ribs long and slow in a moist environment—then the meat will fall off the bone. Yes, they are essentially a by-product and would normally be thrown away, but we are now able to turn them into high-end cooking. All over the Southern states there are cooking competitions focused on ribs, and they spend hours—sometimes days—perfecting their recipes. I have tried to make mine a little more user-friendly so they are easy to cook, but no less delicious. – Phil

Braised pork shoulder with dried blueberries & elderberries

I USE ELDERBERRIES THAT I DRY MYSELF AND IT'S A PERFECT WAY OF KEEPING THEM FOR THE WINTER MONTHS. I HAVE NOT SEEN THEM AVAILABLE TO PURCHASE COMMERCIALLY YET. HOWEVER, IF YOU DON'T HAVE ELDERBERRIES, ANY DRIED RED FRUIT WILL DO. EIGHT HEADS WILL PRODUCE ABOUT ¾LB FRESH BERRIES, AND ONCE DRIED THEY WILL REDUCE IN VOLUME BY ABOUT HALF. I HAVE SOME AT HOME THAT ARE A YEAR OLD. TO DRY THE BERRIES, SPREAD THEM OUT ON A NON-STICK BAKING SHEET AND PLACE IN A VERY COOL OVEN, SAY 225°F, FOR ABOUT 6–7 HOURS. YOU CAN USE A DEHYDRATOR TO DRY THEM IN LESS TIME. THE SAME PROCESS APPLIES TO DRYING FRESH BLUEBERRIES, BUT YOU CAN BUY SEMI-DRIED BLUEBERRIES FROM SUPERMARKETS THAT ARE PRETTY GOOD. ONE OTHER TIP I PICKED UP IN HUNGARY—NEVER ADD PAPRIKA TO HOT OIL, AS IT WILL BURN, TURN BITTER, AND LOSE ITS PERFUME. IF YOU CAN, ALWAYS ADD ONCE ALL THE LIQUID HAS GONE IN.

Serves 4   Preparation time 20 minutes   Cooking time about 2 hours, plus standing

¼ cup vegetable oil
1 large onion, very finely chopped
2¼lb boneless pork shoulder, rind and fat removed, cut into 1¼in pieces
3 tablespoons all-purpose flour
¾ cup Madeira
¾ cup water
1 pork or chicken bouillon cube, crumbled
2 tablespoons sugar
1½ tablespoons smoked paprika
2 tablespoons dried elderberries
2 tablespoons dried blueberries
3 tablespoons pearl barley
salt and freshly ground black pepper

TO SERVE
1 cup thick Greek yogurt
6 tablespoons chopped fresh flat-leaf parsley

✱ Preheat the oven to 325°F.

✱ Put a large ovenproof pan with a tight-fitting lid on the stove and heat the vegetable oil over low heat. Add the onion and cook for 5 minutes to soften slightly.

✱ Mix the pork and flour together well in a bowl. Add to the pan and brown all over, then add the Madeira, water, and bouillon cube and mix well. Stir in the sugar, paprika, dried berries, and barley.

✱ Season well with salt and pepper, mix thoroughly, and just bring to a boil. Immediately cover the pan with the lid, then transfer to the oven and cook for 1 hour 45 minutes.

✱ Remove from the oven and let stand for 20 minutes. Stir in the yogurt and serve scattered with the chopped parsley. It's as simple as that.

Roast pork with white wine, fresh orange juice & oregano

I FIRST COOKED THIS DISH SOME 20 YEARS AGO, AND THE COMBINATION OF FRESH ORANGE AND PUNGENT OREGANO WORKS VERY WELL INDEED WITH PORK. I ALSO REVEAL HERE HOW TO ACHIEVE PERFECT CRACKLING EVERY TIME—IT REALLY IS VERY STRAIGHTFORWARD. ALL YOU NEED TO SERVE WITH THIS DISH IS A LARGE BOWL OF NEW POTATOES AND SOME BROCCOLINI OR EVEN A FEW ASPARAGUS SPEARS.

Serves 6   Preparation time 20 minutes   Cooking time 1 hour 40 minutes, plus resting

2^1/$_4$lb boneless pork shoulder, tied
salt and freshly ground black pepper

SAUCE
^{3}/$_4$ cup dry white wine
^{1}/$_2$ chicken bouillon cube, crumbled (to add a little extra flavor to the sauce)
1 cup fresh orange juice
2 teaspoons sugar
2 teaspoons fresh or 1 tablespoon dried oregano
1 heaping tablespoon cornstarch or arrowroot

✱ Preheat the oven to 375°F.

✱ Season the pork well with salt and pepper, then place on a piece of scrunched-up foil in a roasting pan and pop in the oven. I normally cook this size cut for about 1 hour 20 minutes.

✱ Remove the roasting pan from the oven. Cut off the strings around the meat, remove all the crackling, and place, inner-side up, on a baking sheet. Cover the meat with foil and let rest for another 20 minutes before you eat. This helps the meat relax and become a lot juicier.

✱ While the meat is resting, place the baking sheet with the crackling in the oven, turn the oven up to 425°F, and cook until it turns crispy and well browned. This should take about 20 minutes.

✱ Meanwhile, pour off all the fat from the roasting pan, add the wine, and swirl around to remove any crispy bits from the bottom. Spoon into a saucepan and bring to a boil. Add the bouillon cube, orange juice, sugar, and oregano, then bring back to a boil. Cook for about 5 minutes to reduce slightly and for the bouillon cube to dissolve, then re-season.

✱ Blend the cornstarch or arrowroot with a little cold water until smooth, then stir into a boiling sauce—it will thicken immediately. Keep warm and covered.

✱ To serve, slice the pork, spoon over a little of the sauce, and top with a piece of crackling.

Roasted pork shoulder with sauerkraut, cider vinegar & mustard

ONE OF SIMON'S GREAT IDEAS, THE SUCCULENCE THAT COMES FROM BRINING THE MEAT FIRST MAKES A MASSIVE DIFFERENCE AND IS REALLY WORTHWHILE. THIS CUT ALSO PARTICULARLY LENDS ITSELF TO ROASTING WITH A VERY SMALL AMOUNT OF LIQUID. THE CARAWAY AND TARRAGON, TWO FLAVORS VERY MUCH USED IN GERMAN CURES, COMPLETE THE DISH PERFECTLY. SO DELICIOUS—YOU CAN'T STOP EATING IT!

Serves 4   Preparation time 25 minutes, plus 12 hours brining   Cooking time 2 hours

BRINE
2 cups water
3 tablespoons cooking salt
2 garlic cloves, crushed
1 tablespoon caraway seeds
1 sprig of fresh thyme
1 teaspoon freshly ground black pepper
1 tablespoon brown sugar

2¼lb rolled pork shoulder
2 tablespoons vegetable oil
2 medium onions, finely chopped
2 garlic cloves, chopped
2 teaspoons caraway seeds
3 tablespoons Dijon or sweet mustard
½ cup cider vinegar
½ cup pork or strong chicken stock (or 2 bouillon cubes)
14oz jar sauerkraut, drained well
salt and freshly ground black pepper
1 tablespoon cornstarch or arrowroot
2 tablespoons roughly chopped fresh tarragon

* Make the brine according to the instructions on page 45. Soak the pork in the brine (make sure it is covered) for 12 hours or overnight, then dry off with paper towels before roasting. Rinse the meat well.

* Preheat the oven to 375°F.

* Heat a tablespoon of vegetable oil in a deep, lidded pan big enough to hold the pork. Add the onions, garlic, and caraway seeds and soften for 10 minutes, but do not brown.

* Next add the mustard, vinegar, stock, and sauerkraut and season well with pepper. Bring to a boil and check the seasoning, adding salt if necessary (there will already be some from the sauerkraut and the bouillon cubes).

* Add the brined pork and cover with a tight fitting lid or foil. Simmer for 5 minutes, then transfer into the preheated oven. Cook for 1 hour 30 minutes.

* Remove from the oven and take off the lid. The aroma will be amazing. Carefully lift out the pork using two forks and place in a bowl. The meat should be soft and yielding but not falling apart. Remove the strings and carefully slice off the skin. Wrap the meat tightly in foil and set aside to rest. Place the skin on a foil-lined baking sheet and put back in the oven, skin side down. Increase the heat to 425°F and cook until the skin is nice and crispy, about 15–20 minutes.

* Meanwhile, strain the sauerkraut/onion mixture and reboil the stock that's left. I sometimes thicken it slightly by adding 1 tablespoon cornstarch or arrowroot mixed with 3 tablespoons cold water. Finally, add the chopped fresh tarragon.

* Serve the pork thickly sliced with the sauerkraut and tarragon stock.

My fragrant pork vindaloo

SOME PEOPLE THINK OF VINDALOO AS A VERY HOT CURRY, WHICH CAN CERTAINLY BE THE CASE AT TIMES, BUT IT SHOULD IN FACT BE A FRAGRANT DISH, MILD YET PUNGENT IN CHARACTER. THIS REQUIRES A COMPLEX BALANCE OF FLAVORINGS, AS THE LENGTHY LIST OF INGREDIENTS BELOW SHOWS. BUT DON'T BE PUT OFF—THE SECRET IS SIMPLY TO ENSURE THAT THE SPICE MIX IS CAREFULLY PREPARED FOR THE BEST RESULTS.

Serves 4–6   Preparation time 1 hour standing/soaking   Cooking time about 2 hours

3¼lb pork shoulder or butt (I like to include
    some extra fat), cut into large cubes
¼ cup sugar
2 tablespoons salt

SAUCE
4 large dried red chiles
2 tablespoons ground cumin
2 tablespoons ground coriander
2 teaspoons coriander seeds, crushed
5 teaspoons garam masala
2 teaspoons ground fenugreek
6 tablespoons vegetable oil
6 garlic cloves, chopped
2 tablespoons finely chopped fresh ginger
3 onions, finely sliced

8 ripe tomatoes, chopped
2 tablespoons tomato paste
2 tablespoons smoked paprika
20 curry leaves
1¼ cups tomato juice
2 tablespoons cider vinegar
a pinch or two of sugar, to taste
salt and freshly ground black pepper

✱ Preheat the oven to 350°F.

✱ Put the cubed pork into a bowl, add the sugar and salt, and mix well. Cover and let stand in a cool place for 1 hour, mixing occasionally.

✱ Meanwhile, place the chiles in ½ cup warm water and let soak for 30 minutes. Drain the chiles, reserving the water, and then chop them up to make a paste—a mortar and pestle is good here, but still chop them finely first.

✱ Gently toast the cumin and ground and crushed coriander in a large frying pan, then stir in the garam masala and fenugreek off the heat and let cool.

✱ After 1 hour, rinse the pork well in a colander to remove all the sugar and salt, then pat dry with paper towels.

✱ Heat half the oil in a large ovenproof pan with a tight-fitting lid over low heat, add the garlic and ginger, and cook until well colored. Then add the onions and brown well.

✱ Next add the tomatoes, tomato paste, paprika, curry leaves, tomato juice, vinegar, sugar, and salt and pepper. Stir well and then add the spices, chile paste, and reserved water and cook down for about 8–10 minutes until the sauce is nice and thick.

✱ Heat the remaining oil in a separate large pan and brown the pork quickly, in batches if necessary, then add to the sauce. Check the seasoning. Bring to a simmer, then cover with the lid, pop into the oven, and cook for 1 hour 30 minutes. Check at that point—the meat should be tender and succulent, but not overcooked. When ready, serve with boiled rice.

Crispy pork salad with maple syrup, pork rinds & lemon

THIS IS A GREAT DISH THAT MAKES GROUND PORK GO A LONG WAY. THE SPICES, COUPLED WITH THE RELATIVELY HIGH FAT CONTENT OF THE PORK, HELP TO MAKE A REALLY TASTY SALAD, WITH THE RECOOKED PORK RINDS ADDING A NICE SWEET, CRISPY EDGE.

Serves 4   Preparation time 20 minutes   Cooking time 20–25 minutes

PORK RINDS
7oz pork rinds or chicharonnes (alternatively, crispy bacon pieces are just as good), store-bought or see page 188
¼ cup maple syrup

1lb 2oz ground pork, slightly fattier is better—any cut from the shoulder is perfect
1 teaspoon salt
1 tablespoon Chinese five-spice powder
½ tablespoon ground cumin
2 tablespoons vegetable oil
salt and freshly ground black pepper

DRESSING
¼ cup honey
finely grated zest and juice of 2 large lemons
3 tablespoons olive oil
2 tablespoons dark soy sauce
2 tablespoons *nam pla* (Thai fish sauce)
1 teaspoon sugar

SALAD
1 head Romaine or Iceberg lettuce, very finely shredded
1 small bunch of radishes, washed, green shoots left on and thinly sliced
1 small bag watercress

✱ Preheat the oven to 400°F.

✱ Put the pork rinds into a non-stick ovenproof frying pan, spoon in the maple syrup, and mix well. Pop into the oven and cook for 10 minutes, stirring occasionally, until nicely browned and all the maple syrup has been soaked up. Watch closely, as it will easily burn.

✱ Remove the pan from the oven and let the rinds cool. They will stick together while cooling, so break them up.

✱ Meanwhile, put the pork, salt, five-spice, and cumin into a bowl and mix well.

✱ Heat a large non-stick frying pan on the stove and add the vegetable oil, then the pork mixture. As the pork heats up, break it up with a wooden spoon or spatula until the meat is all loose and cooking nicely. Be careful here—it's a bit tedious, but well worth the effort to break up all the small strands of pork. You will find that the meat starts to

boil, but this is no problem and quite normal, especially with vacuum-packed meat. Let the pork boil, stirring all the time. After a few minutes, the water will evaporate and the pork will start to cook in the small amount of oil and the fat from the meat.

✱ After another 5 minutes, the meat will brown nice and evenly. Once really browned and crispy, spoon it into a colander over a bowl to catch the oil and fat. Sprinkle with a little salt and pepper.

✱ Next make the dressing. Put all the dressing ingredients into a bowl. Add a little salt and pepper and whisk it all together well.

✱ Put the lettuce, radishes, and watercress into a salad bowl, spoon in the dressing, and mix well but carefully. Add the warm crispy pork and again mix well but carefully.

✱ Pile the salad onto four serving plates and top with the crunchy pork rinds. Serve immediately.

Succulent pork with plums, sugar & onions

I HAVE USED THIS RECIPE BEFORE IN MY OTHER BOOKS, BUT IT'S SO GOOD THAT I JUST HAVE TO REPEAT IT. YES, BEFORE I GET READERS' LETTERS, YOU DO ADD THE PORK TO THE BUBBLING CARAMEL. IT REALLY IS SO EASY AND THE PLUMS MAKE A GREAT SAUCE ONCE COOKED DOWN. ANY FRUIT WOULD WORK WELL HERE, SO TRY APPLES, PEARS, MANGO, AND EVEN KIWI FRUIT.

Serves 4–6   Preparation time 15 minutes   Cooking time about 2 hours 15 minutes

1/2 cup sugar
21/2lb pork shoulder, rind removed but fat left on, cut into 21/4in chunks
salt and freshly ground black pepper
2 onions, roughly chopped
3 tablespoons Worcestershire sauce
3 tablespoons dark soy sauce
1/4 cup lemon juice
2 chicken bouillon cubes, crumbled
12 ripe plums, halved and pitted
7oz blood sausage, sliced
13/4 cups frozen peas, cooked
1 tablespoon cornstarch or arrowroot

* Preheat the oven to 350°F.

* Put a large ovenproof pan with a tight-fitting lid on the stove and heat the sugar in the pan over medium heat.

* Meanwhile, dry the pork chunks on paper towels—the drier they are, the better. Season the pork well with salt and pepper.

* Stir the melting sugar with a wooden spoon until you have a thick caramel. If the sugar starts to burn, you can add a small amount of water, which will slow the process. Add the pork to the caramel, mix well, and cook for 2–3 minutes.

* Stir in the onion, sauces, lemon juice, and bouillon cubes and mix well. Bring to a boil, then add the plums, sausage slices, and a little salt, and again mix well.

* Bring back to a boil, then cover with the lid and transfer to the oven. Cook for 2 hours and then check to see if the meat is cooked through and very tender.

* Once the meat is ready, stir in the peas. Mix the cornstarch or arrowroot with 2–3 tablespoons water, stir into the pan, and warm through on the stove. Serve with boiled, slightly crushed new potatoes.

SOUS VIDE

Sous vide is the French for "under vacuum" and is a method of cooking meat or vegetables for longer periods of time and at much lower temperatures than normal. It ensures that whatever you are cooking achieves the same level of doneness at the center as it does on the outside. Meat in particular remains exceptionally juicy if cooked in this way. It has become extremely popular over the last few years and if used in the right context is a fantastic way to cook meat, especially pork. I was shown the basics of this method on a visit to Belgium about 12 years ago with one of my ingredients suppliers. It was absolutely fascinating and I subsequently started using some of the techniques in my own business.

During the summer there is nothing nicer, weather permitting, than eating barbecued spare ribs with a wonderful sticky sauce. However, when simply grilled over charcoal for a short amount of time, spare ribs can be one of the toughest things you could ever put in your mouth. Precooking them using the sous-vide method will give you some of the most tender spare ribs imaginable. You will need access to a vacuum sealer and a sous-vide water bath or steam combination oven to do it by the book, but there is a way you can do it at home without either. – Simon

St. Louis cut spare ribs

I FIRST HAD THESE AT A RIB SHACK IN ST. LUCIA WHILE ON VACATION, AND AMAZING IS THE ONLY DESCRIPTION I CAN GIVE THEM. USING THE SOUS-VIDE METHOD OF COOKING IS THE CLOSEST I HAVE COME TO RECREATING THAT MELT-IN-THE-MOUTH TEXTURE.

Serves 4–5   Preparation time 8–10 hours

1 rack St. Louis cut spare ribs
  (these are cut from the belly so are rectangular in shape, making every rib the same length and thickness)

* On the inner rib side of the rack is a very fine, thin, gossamer-like skin coating the ribs. This must be removed before cooking or the ribs will be tough as old boots. It's very easy to remove—take a sharp knife and, from the top of the last rib bone, scrape the skin away from the cut bone end. It should come away easily. Once you have enough to pull away, get a piece of paper towel, grab ahold of the skin, and pull. It will tear away easily along the whole inside of the rib cage. Then continue with your chosen method below.

THE PROPER METHOD

* Place the rack in a vacuum cooking bag and vacuum seal. Place the bag in a sous vide water bath or steam combination oven and cook for 8–10 hours at 160°F.

* After cooking, chill very quickly in iced water and refrigerate until you are ready to grill or broil them (see page 34).

THE IMPROVISED METHOD

* Wrap the rib rack tightly in foil or plastic wrap and place on a roasting rack in a roasting pan with ½in water in the bottom. Wrap the pan and rib package tightly in foil to create a kind of tent.

* Set your oven to its lowest temperature—175–200°F if possible—and cook for 8–10 hours. After cooking, refrigerate until you are ready to grill or broil them (see page 34).

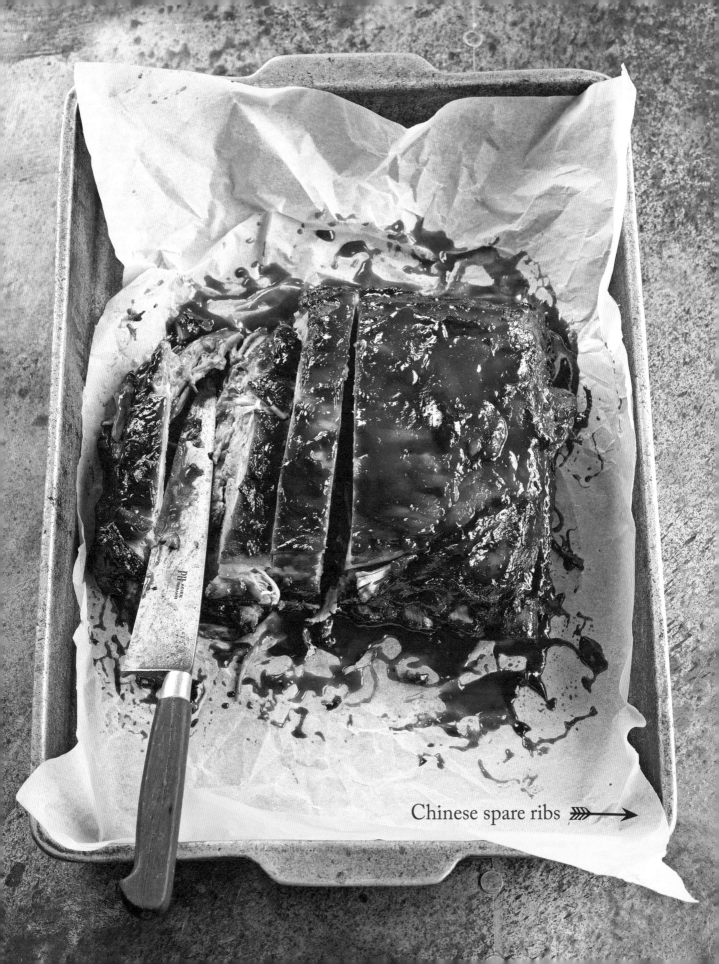

Chinese spare ribs →

Chinese spare ribs

A STAPLE IN OUR HOUSE, I LOVE THE SPICES ON THESE RIBS. AGAIN, THIS IS A VERY EASY DISH TO MAKE, BUT MAKE SURE YOU KEEP COATING THE RIBS WELL WITH THE MARINADE. I USE SPARE RIBS THAT ARE CUT FROM THE BELLY SO THAT THEY HAVE MUCH MORE MEAT ON THEM, AS OPPOSED TO THE BABY BACK ONES CUT FROM THE TOP OF THE RIBS TOWARD THE LOIN.

Serves 4   Preparation time 2 hours or overnight marinating   Cooking time 1–2 hours simmering, 45 minutes–1 hour roasting

2¼lb whole racks large spare ribs, full of meat
1 beef bouillon cube, crumbled

MARINADE
6 tablespoons ketchup
¼ cup hoisin sauce
¼ cup dark soy sauce
2 tablespoons honey
2 tablespoons Chinese rice wine or dry sherry
1 tablespoon sweet chili sauce
1 teaspoon sesame oil
2 garlic cloves, grated
1½ tablespoons grated fresh ginger
¼ teaspoon Chinese five-spice powder

✱ On the inner rib side of the rack is a very fine, thin, gossamer-like skin coating the ribs. This must be removed before cooking or the ribs will be tough as old boots. It's very easy to remove—take a sharp knife and, from the top of the last rib bone, scrape the skin away from the cut bone end. It should come away easily. Once you have enough to pull away, get a piece of paper towel, grab ahold of the skin, and pull. It will tear away easily along the whole inside of the rib cage.

✱ Put the whole racks into a large pan, cover with water, and add the bouillon cube. Bring to a boil, then cover with a lid, reduce the heat, and simmer gently for 1–2 hours, or until the meat is almost falling off the bone, adding more water if necessary.

✱ Remove from the heat and let the racks cool in the stock. Drain the ribs, pat dry, and place in a large, resealable plastic food bag.

✱ Mix the marinade ingredients together thoroughly, reserve half, and add the other half to the racks in the bag, coating the ribs well. Seal the bag and leave in the fridge for 2 hours, or preferably overnight.

✱ Preheat the oven to 375°F.

✱ Lay the racks, meaty-side up, on a sheet of foil in a shallow roasting dish and coat with the reserved marinade. Cover the ribs with a tent of foil and roast for about 45 minutes–1 hour, spooning over the marinade occasionally so that the ribs are nicely glazed, uncovering for the last 15 minutes of cooking.

✱ Remove the dish from the oven and let the ribs cool for 10–15 minutes before serving.

Barbecue spare ribs

BABY BACK RIBS ARE SO DELICIOUS, THEY HAVE TO BE IN THIS BOOK. BE CAREFUL NOT TO OVERCOOK THEM, OTHERWISE THE MEAT WILL LITERALLY FALL OFF THE BONE. PREPARE AND COOK THESE IN THE SAME MANNER AS THE CHINESE-STYLE RIBS (LEFT). AS WITH ALL THE RIB RECIPES, THEY CAN BE FINISHED ON THE GRILL IN THE SUMMER MONTHS.

Serves 4   Preparation time 2 hours or overnight marinating, plus cooling
Cooking time 1–2 hours simmering, 45 minutes–1 hour roasting

2¼lb whole racks baby back pork ribs
1 beef bouillon cube, crumbled

MARINADE
1 tablespoon Dijon mustard
½ teaspoon smoked paprika
6 tablespoons ketchup
¼ cup fresh lemon juice
¼ cup teriyaki sauce
¼ cup dark brown sugar
1 teaspoon Worcestershire sauce

Indian-style ribs

IT IS QUITE UNUSUAL TO SEE THESE RIBS, AS PORK IS NOT EATEN IN MUCH OF INDIA, BUT GOA IN THE WEST IS THE EXCEPTION, OWING TO ITS PORTUGUESE COLONIAL HERITAGE. THE MIX OF SPICES REALLY WORKS WELL, AND THE KETCHUP AND MANGO ADD A NICE SWEET EDGE TO THE WHOLE DISH. THIS AND THE OTHER RIB RECIPES ALL FREEZE BEAUTIFULLY. PREPARE AND COOK THESE IN THE SAME MANNER AS THE CHINESE-STYLE RIBS (LEFT).

Serves 4   Preparation time 2 hours or overnight marinating, plus cooling
Cooking time 1–2 hours simmering, 45 minutes–1 hour roasting

2¼lb whole racks pork ribs—baby back, loin or spare
1 beef bouillon cube, crumbled

MARINADE
6 tablespoons vegetable oil
6 tablespoons red or white wine vinegar
6 tablespoons ketchup
1 tablespoon mango chutney
1½ tablespoons finely grated fresh ginger
1 tablespoon grated garlic
1 tablespoon ground coriander
3 teaspoons cumin powder
1 teaspoon chile powder

Pulled pork

FOR A SANDWICH, FORGET ROAST PORK—THIS IS WITHOUT QUESTION THE ONLY OPTION.

Serves 10–12   Preparation time 10 minutes   Cooking time 12 or 14 hours

1 pork butt, weighing about 4½–5½lb

SPICE RUB
2 tablespoons salt
2 tablespoons sugar
2 tablespoons brown sugar
2 tablespoons ground cumin
2 tablespoons freshly ground black pepper
1 tablespoon cayenne pepper
¼ cup paprika

THE PROPER METHOD
✱ Cover the meat with the spice rub, place in a vacuum cooking bag, and vacuum seal. Place the bag in a sous-vide water bath or steam combination oven and cook for 12 hours at 175°F.

✱ After cooking, remove the pork from the bag and pull apart into bite-sized strips. Slather with the barbecue sauce (marinade) on page 35 and enjoy.

THE IMPROVISED METHOD
✱ Once you have covered the meat with the spice rub, wrap it tightly in foil or plastic wrap, and place on a roasting rack in a roasting pan with ½in water in the bottom. Wrap the pan and meat package tightly in foil to create a kind of tent.

✱ Set your oven to its lowest temperature—175–200°F if possible—and cook for 14 hours.

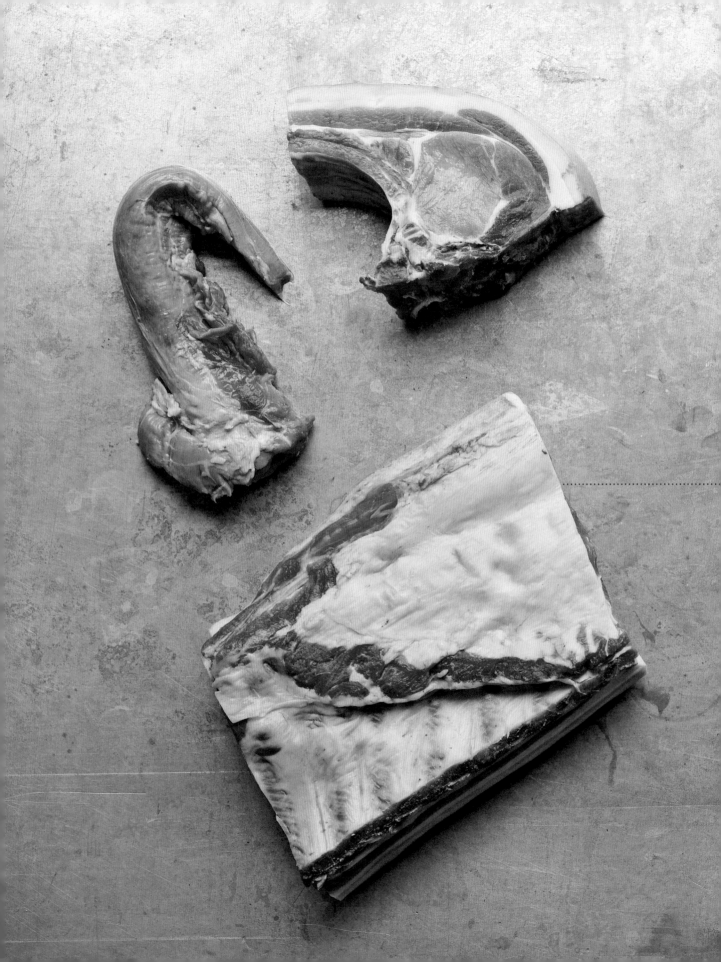

CHAPTER 2 Belly, loin & chops

As with any four-legged animal, the middle rear of the pig is where you will find what chefs and butchers call the "prime" cuts. Loins are cooked or cured whole; the rib end is cut into thick pork chops, and comes, if you're lucky, with a nice layer of fat and a little kidney (my father's favorite). The belly, now a staple in any good kitchen, is cooked or cured in a variety of ways to produce everything from pancetta to rillons, chunks of salted pork gently sautéed in their own fat. Pork loin, seen as the best and priciest cut, is tasty either roasted whole or turned into scallopini and sautéed. It needs careful attention, though, as it can dry out very quickly—it's worth remembering that lean pork has less fat per pound than cottage cheese.

The belly and loin can also be made into what seems like an endless variety of cooked and cured products. Take, for instance, bacon, probably the world's most popular pork product. Whether you want to produce slab or sliced bacon, the permutations are vast (see Chapter 4). The recipes here are some of Simon's favorites, although for my own breakfast or in a sandwich or roll with a free-range egg I'd opt for green (unsmoked) bacon any day of the week. Other preparations from the loin include lomo (see page 81), a Spanish speciality that is salt cured then air dried, and is delicious sliced and served at room temperature with a chilled glass of white wine—the sweet, rosy cured loin is perfectly offset by the creamy, salty fat. Lardo, or speck, is another Italian speciality that is popular around the world, and is made by removing the thick fatback from loins and then curing it in salt and also sometimes herbs and pepper. A while ago, I spent a long time working on and off in a factory in Italy. When we finished our day's work we would walk back to the hotel, stopping off for a quick drink. The bar owner would always offer a board of cured meats and cheese to nibble on. It could be a light prosciutto-style cured leg or a small selection of salami, but my favorite was speck—a 1½in thick cured piece of creamy fat, sliced gossamer thin and served with a little cracked pepper. I remember the taste, texture, and flavor even to this day. The curing recipes that follow are all very simple and I would encourage you to give them a try. – Phil

Simple pork & raisin terrine

A SIMPLE TERRINE LIKE THIS IS REALLY VERY EASY TO MAKE. MANY A TIME IN FRANCE I HAVE STOPPED FOR A LIGHT LUNCH OR SNACK, AND WHICHEVER REGION YOU ARE IN YOU WILL ALWAYS FIND A LOCAL TERRINE OR PÂTÉ OF SOME SORT. I HAVE FOUND THAT INTRODUCING A LITTLE REDUCED MEAT JUICE OR ALCOHOL ALWAYS BRINGS OUT A DEEPER FLAVOR. BRANDY AND SHERRY ARE USED FAIRLY OFTEN, BUT HERE I'VE OPTED FOR MADEIRA. MANY STORES NOW SELL THE CLASSIC TERRINE DISH (MINE IS 4 X 10½IN AND 3IN DEEP), BUT ANY DEEP, LIDDED OVENPROOF DISH WILL DO.

Makes 1 terrine   Preparation time 30 minutes   Cooking time 1 hour 30–45 minutes

4 shallots, finely chopped
3 garlic cloves, finely chopped
½ cup Madeira
2 tablespoons roughly chopped fresh thyme leaves
¾ cup well-reduced and well-flavored pork or chicken stock
12 slices thick-cut bacon
1lb 10oz rindless pork belly, cut into large cubes for grinding/chopping, or ground
3½oz cured pork belly, pancetta, or bacon offcuts, cut into small cubes
5½oz pork fatback, cut into small cubes
⅓ cup raisins, soaked in boiling water for 20 minutes and water gently squeezed out
salt and freshly ground black pepper
vegetable oil, for oiling

✱ Preheat the oven to 300°F. Put the shallots, garlic, Madeira, thyme, and stock together into a saucepan and bring to a boil. Reduce the heat and simmer for 10–15 minutes until you have a thick gravy, then let cool.

✱ Line a lidded terrine dish with the bacon slices, overlapping them slightly.

✱ Grind or roughly chop the pork belly cubes, if not already ground, and put in a large bowl. Add the cured pork, fatback, raisins, and the cooled gravy and mix really well. Season with pepper and a little salt, taking into consideration the salt from the bacon in the mix and also lining the terrine.

✱ Pack the mixture into the terrine, making sure there are no air pockets. Fold the bacon over in a crisscross fashion. Lay a double-thickness piece of foil on a cutting board and lightly oil on one side. Place the oiled side onto the bacon, press down firmly, and secure. Then place the lid on the terrine.

✱ Stand the terrine in a deep baking pan and half-fill with boiling water. You may need to add more water during the cooking period. Carefully place the pan in the oven and cook for 1 hour 20–30 minutes.

✱ To check if it's cooked, insert a skewer or small knife into the meat—the juices should run clear. When cooked, remove from the oven and lift out of the water, then place on a clean baking sheet. Lift off the lid and you will see that the terrine has reduced slightly and come away from the sides of the dish. Wrap a piece of cardboard the same size as the terrine in plastic wrap and place on top of the foil.

✱ Let cool for 30 minutes, then place a bag of sugar or a couple of unopened cans on top of the card—this will press the terrine and make it easier to cut when cold. Chill well in the fridge, probably best overnight.

✱ The next day, place the terrine in a large bowl, fill with warm water around the outside of the terrine, and leave for 5 minutes. This will release the jelly and allow you to remove the terrine from its dish by turning it upside down and helping it out a little.

✱ Slice and serve with buttered and toasted seeded bread.

Juicy pork cutlets
with warm winter coleslaw

I LIKE THIS DISH PURELY BECAUSE OF THE AMAZING DIFFERENCE THE BRINE MAKES. YES, YOU ONLY NEED 20 MINUTES TO COMPLETELY CHANGE THE STRUCTURE OF THE MEAT AND IT WILL BE FULL OF FLAVOR AND REALLY JUICY. WINTER COLESLAW IS ANOTHER LOVELY SALAD, AND IF YOU CAN LEAVE IT TO MARINATE, ALL THE BETTER, AS THE VEGETABLES WILL SOFTEN BUT STILL RETAIN A NICE CRUNCH.

Serves 4   Preparation time 35 minutes, including cooling/standing   Cooking time 10–15 minutes

BRINE
2 tablespoons sugar
1 tablespoon salt
1¼ cups water
2 tablespoons olive oil

4 boneless, rindless pork cutlets, ¾in thick

SALAD
¼ white cabbage, very finely sliced
¼ red cabbage, very finely sliced
1 large carrot, peeled and very finely sliced
4 scallions, very finely sliced on the diagonal
1 small bunch roughly chopped fresh cilantro

DRESSING
3 tablespoons walnut oil
3 tablespoons sherry vinegar
2 tablespoons olive oil
2 teaspoons sugar
1 garlic clove, crushed to a paste
½ teaspoon salt
½ teaspoon ground white pepper
pinch of red pepper flakes with seeds

* Put the brine ingredients into a stainless steel saucepan. Dissolve the sugar and salt slowly in the water over low heat, add the oil, then bring to a boil. Remove from the heat and let cool, then top off with cold water to the original quantity of brine (1½ cups).

* Place the pork cutlets in a glass, ceramic, or stainless steel bowl. Pour in the cold brine and mix well, then let stand in a cool place for 20–30 minutes.

* Meanwhile, prepare the salad ingredients. I find the best way is to finely slice the root vegetables using a food-processor fitted with a fine slicer attachment. Put the sliced vegetables in a bowl with the cilantro.

* Combine all the dressing ingredients in a bowl and mix well. Transfer to a saucepan and gently warm; do not boil. Pour over the salad and mix really well, then leave in a warm place to marinate.

* Heat the olive oil in a frying pan. Drain the pork well, then pat dry with paper towels. Pan-fry gently for 3–4 minutes on each side. Serve with the warm coleslaw and a few boiled new potatoes.

COOKING IN A WOOD-BURNING OVEN

There is no set recipe to cooking in a wood-burning oven, as much depends on which type you have, so what follows is a list of general points and advice. My own oven is wood-fired, although gas is also good and far more controllable.

LOGS Different woods burn for different times and, most importantly, at different heat levels. If seasoned correctly, cherry, oak, beech, etc., will all burn at roughly the same heat and for the same length of time, so these are what I use. I steer clear of resin woods such as pine as they impart an awful flavor and smoke. Green (freshly cut) wood is difficult to burn as it's full of sap. The only time I use a little green wood is if I want to produce a bit more of a smoke flavor. All wood must be seasoned or dried correctly. I use a redundant greenhouse for drying my wood. I cut in the late winter, split any green, then store in the spring and summer so it dries perfectly. I normally work a year ahead of myself so I can cook all year round. I then split my logs into $1^3/_4$ foot lengths, say 1 foot across, as I find these burn well and evenly for my oven, giving a constant heat, although I use chunkier logs if I want a lot more heat for steaks or pizzas.

LIGHTING THE FIRE I use small bundles of kindling and paper to get the fire going (never lighters or lighter fluid) then thinner pieces of wood, the same length, to keep the fire at a constant temperature, for when cooking larger pieces of meat or whole suckling pigs (see below). When the embers are red-hot they only need a few pieces of wood to keep them going. I light my fire roughly 45 minutes to an hour in advance so the oven reaches the right heat and is stable. My builder, Paul, told me that once the flue and bricks are warm, the smoke will disappear, and generally speaking it does, so don't be too worried about smoke at the start. Another reason to wait for the oven to warm up.

COOKING I tend to move my fire around every time I cook, but have found that cooking to one side tends to be a good starting point. Once the oven is warm, you need small amounts of thinner wood to keep the temperature constant—the most important part of this cooking technique. Making the fire at the rear of the oven is good for larger cuts or pieces of meat that need to be cooked for longer as this means they can be positioned away from the heat. If I'm cooking pizzas, steaks, chops, or cutlets I make the fire directly in the middle, then once the oven has reached the required heat I push the embers to the rear of the oven and bake on the very hot stones.

EQUIPMENT I use a large wire brush for brushing away hot embers, plus a couple of homemade pokers and rectangular trays for catching fatty deposits when roasting meat. Probably the most important of all, though, is a laser thermometer—useful for checking the temperature all around the oven and also of the food you are cooking.

That's pretty much it. It's a bit like learning to fly fish—it takes a day to learn, but a lifetime to master. It's all a matter of practice and seeing what works for you. The best piece of advice is to keep checking the temperature and the fire.

Suckling pig

I TEND TO USE A SMALLER PIG, 18–22LB. I DON'T SCORE THE FLESH, JUST SEASON IT WELL, BOTH INSIDE AND OUT, THEN PLACE ON A TRAY TO CATCH ALL THE JUICES. DURING COOKING, MOVE THE TRAY AROUND AND ALSO TURN THE PIG AND BASTE AT REGULAR INTERVALS TO ENSURE AN EVEN COOK. THE IMPORTANT THING IS TO KEEP A CAREFUL EYE ON THE PIG AND TO COOK IT LONG AND SLOW. IF YOU DO SO, YOU REALLY CAN'T GO WRONG.

Flash-fried pork skirt with cucumber, tomato & chile pickle

THE SKIRT STEAK ON A PIG IS SIMILAR TO THE BAVETTE ON A BEEF CARCASS: IT'S A DELICATE CUT FROM INSIDE THE LEG THAT GETS LARGELY FORGOTTEN. IT'S SO TENDER, LEAN, AND JUICY THAT THE LESS YOU DO WITH IT, THE BETTER, IN MY VIEW. YOU CAN FLASH-FRY IT, AS I DO IN THIS RECIPE, OR SIMPLY GRILL, BUT YOU MUST MAKE SURE YOU DO NOT OVERCOOK IT. THE BEST THING TO DO IS TO HALF COOK IT, MAKING NOTE OF HOW LONG YOU DID SO, THEN REMOVE IT FROM THE HEAT SOURCE, LIGHTLY COVER WITH A PIECE OF FOIL, AND LET REST FOR THE EXACT SAME TIME. IT WILL BE COOKED TO PERFECTION. NEITHER OVERCOOKED OR UNDERCOOKED—JUST PERFECT! HERE I SERVE IT WITH A CRUNCHY, SHARP CUCUMBER AND TOMATO SALAD, MARINATED WITH A LITTLE CHILE.

Serves 4   Preparation time 20 minutes   Cooking time 6-8 minutes maximum

$^3/_4$ cup rice wine vinegar
1 large cucumber, finely chopped
4 ripe tomatoes, finely chopped
4 small scallions, finely chopped
6 tablespoons olive oil
salt and freshly ground black pepper
pinch of sugar
4 x $4^1/_2$–$5^1/_2$oz pieces of pork skirt steak
1 tablespoon unsalted butter
$2^1/_2$ cups spinach leaves

✱ Bring the rice vinegar to a boil, simmer for 3–4 minutes, then cool.

✱ Place the cucumber, tomatoes, scallions, and 4 tablespoons olive oil in a bowl, season with a pinch of black pepper, then add the sugar and vinegar and leave for 20 minutes.

✱ Heat a large frying pan and add the remaining olive oil. Season the skirts really well, add to the hot oil, and cook for 3–4 minutes. Turn over, add the butter, and cook for another 2–3 minutes, basting with the oil and the butter.

✱ Remove from the pan, loosely cover with foil, and let rest in a warm place for 6–7 minutes.

✱ Just before serving, add the spinach leaves to the cucumber and tomato mixture and allow them to wilt slightly.

✱ Pile the salad onto 4 plates and top with the skirt steak. It's as simple as that. If you want to be a bit cheffy, you can cut the skirt across the grain of the meat into 5 or 6 slices.

Porchetta

TRADITIONALLY, PORCHETTA IS A BONELESS SUCKLING PIG SEASONED WITH SALT, HERBS, AND SPICES AND ROASTED IN A WOOD-BURNING OVEN. MY VERSION USES JUST THE MIDDLE OF THE ANIMAL, THE LOIN (THE TISSUE ALONG THE TOP OF THE RIB CAGE) AND BELLY.

Makes 2¼lb   Preparation time 10 minutes   Cooking time 40 minutes, plus 40 minutes resting

2¼lb boneless pork (from the middle)

SPICE RUB
1 tablespoon salt
1 tablespoon fennel seeds, crushed
1 teaspoon coarsely ground black pepper
1 teaspoon dried thyme
1 teaspoon smoked paprika
4 garlic cloves, chopped

✱ Mix all the spice rub ingredients together thoroughly and rub into the meat. Preheat the oven to 400°F.

✱ Roll the belly part into the thicker loin part, tie securely, then score finely with a sharp knife. Roast in the oven for 40 minutes, then remove and let rest for another 40 minutes before serving.

Rillettes

PERHAPS ONE OF THE MOST DECADENT THINGS YOU CAN EAT (WELL I THINK SO ANYWAY), RILLETTES IS SIMILAR TO A PÂTÉ IN THAT YOU CAN SPREAD IT ON BREAD OR TOAST. SINCE IT IS PRESERVED IN THE FAT IT'S COOKED IN, IT ISN'T FOR THE FAINT-HEARTED.

Makes 2¼lb   Preparation time 10 minutes, plus standing   Cooking time 4–5 hours

2¼lb pork butt, cut into strips
7oz pork fatback, cut into small cubes
1 tablespoon cooking salt
1 teaspoon ground white pepper
3 garlic cloves, chopped
1 tablespoon chopped fresh thyme

✱ Mix the meat and fat with all the seasonings in a large bowl, then cover and let stand overnight in the fridge.

✱ Preheat the oven to 275°F.

✱ Pack the meat mixture into a terrine dish or deep, lidded ovenproof dish, cover with the lid, and cook for 4–5 hours until the meat is fork tender.

✱ Once it is cooked, remove the meat from the dish, reserving the fat, and shred with a fork. Press the shredded pork into the cleaned dish.

✱ Put the reserved fat into a pan and gently melt, then pour a thin layer over the rillettes. Chill overnight and enjoy.

Crisp, succulent pork belly with gherkin & shallot dressing

PORK BELLY IS ALL THE RAGE THESE DAYS, PARTLY BECAUSE IT'S CHEAP, EASY TO COOK, AND YOU REALLY HAVE TO GO TO SOME EFFORT TO MESS IT UP. HOWEVER, IT CAN BE A BIT FATTY AND THIS CAN TURN A LOT OF PEOPLE OFF. ONE OF THE BEST WAYS OF AVOIDING THIS IS TO MAKE SURE THE SKIN IS CRISP. HERE IS A SUCCULENT RECIPE, WITH A SHARP RELISH/MAYO TO CUT THE RICHNESS.

Serves 4   Preparation time 25 minutes, plus 12 hours or overnight standing and then chilling
Cooking time about 2 hours 20 minutes

3 tablespoons salt
3$\frac{1}{4}$lb piece of boneless pork belly, rind on
6 garlic cloves, very well crushed
a few sprigs of fresh thyme
about 3$\frac{1}{4}$ cups sunflower oil

DRESSING
$\frac{1}{2}$ cup mayonnaise
6 large gherkins, finely chopped
$\frac{1}{2}$ turnip, peeled and very finely chopped
3 large shallots, very finely chopped
$\frac{1}{4}$ cup chopped fresh flat-leaf parsley
juice of $\frac{1}{2}$ lemon, or to taste
$\frac{1}{2}$ teaspoon freshly ground black pepper

* Rub the salt over the pork, then rub the garlic and thyme in well. Place the pork in a glass dish, cover with plastic wrap, and let stand in the fridge for 12 hours or overnight.

* The following day, preheat the oven to 375°F. Remove the plastic wrap, wash the salt, garlic, and thyme off the pork, pat dry, then place in a small, deep roasting pan just large enough to fit the pork.

* Gently heat the sunflower oil and carefully pour over the pork so that it is submerged. Cover with foil and carefully place the pan in the oven to cook for about 2 hours, or until a knife can pass through the pork easily. The meat should be very soft and almost too difficult to pick up, but not stringy and overcooked. Remove from the oven and let cool.

* Lift out the pork, place rind-side down on a flat plate, and cover with plastic wrap. Press down another plate on top and then chill well.

* When ready to cook, preheat the oven to 425°F.

* Cut the pork into four perfect squares and trim off any ragged edges.

* Heat a dry non-stick ovenproof frying pan, place the pork rind-side down in the pan, and cook until the skin begins to crackle.

* Transfer to the oven and cook for 15 minutes.

* Meanwhile, for the dressing, put the mayo, gherkins, turnip, shallots, and parsley in a bowl and mix really well. Add lemon juice to taste and the black pepper.

* Serve the pork, crispy-side up, with some small florets of broccoli and the dressing.

Juicy pork chops with strawberries & mustard

ALTHOUGH THIS COMBINATION SOUNDS A LITTLE BIZARRE, IT COMES FROM A VERY OLD ENGLISH RECIPE AND IS DELICIOUS, I PROMISE. THE ACID IN THE STRAWBERRY MARINADE BREAKS DOWN THE STRUCTURE OF THE MEAT VERY WELL INDEED, SIMILAR TO THE REACTION OF MARINATING MEAT IN YOGURT, INDIAN STYLE. IT ALSO UTILIZES THOSE VERY SOFT STRAWBERRIES LEFT OVER IN THE BOTTOM OF THE CONTAINER.

Serves 4   Preparation time 20 minutes, plus marinating/cooling   Cooking time 20–25 minutes

MARINADE
1³/₄ cups ripe, juicy strawberries
5 tablespoons olive oil
juice of 2 large lemons
2 tablespoons white wine vinegar
1 tablespoon strawberry jam or other jam
2 teaspoons Dijon mustard
1 small onion, finely chopped
2 garlic cloves, chopped

4 thick pork chops
2 tablespoons olive oil
salt and freshly ground black pepper

✱ For the marinade, wash the strawberries well, then put 1¼ cups into a blender, reserving the rest for later. Add all the remaining marinade ingredients with salt and pepper and blend until smooth.

✱ Strain the purée well to remove the seeds, then adjust the seasoning if necessary.

✱ Using a sharp knife, nick the fat and the rind of each chop, then pierce the meat lightly. Place in a glass or ceramic dish and pour in half the strawberry marinade. Cover and let marinate for 20 minutes at room temperature, or longer in the fridge, but overnight at most.

✱ Put the remaining marinade in a saucepan and cook for 10 minutes—it will thicken up nicely. Let cool.

✱ When ready to cook, preheat the oven to 400°F.

✱ Warm a large ovenproof frying pan on the stove and add the olive oil. Remove the chops or cutlets from their marinade and pat dry with paper towels, then season well with salt and pepper. Add to the warm oil and cook for about 4–5 minutes until lightly browned on the underside.

✱ Turn over, pop into the oven, and cook for 6–8 minutes until cooked through; do not overcook.

✱ Remove from the oven and cover with foil, then leave for 10 minutes to relax.

✱ Chop the reserved strawberries and add to the cooled marinade to make a relish. Serve the pork chops or cutlets with the relish and the Quinoa, Rice & Salted Cashew Salad (see opposite).

Quinoa, rice & salted cashew salad

A NICE NUTTY SALAD THAT WORKS PERFECTLY WITH PORK CHOPS, OR INDEED ANY ROASTED OR GRILLED MEATS. THE KEY THING HERE IS TO NOT OVERCOOK THE QUINOA SO THAT YOU KEEP ITS CRUNCHY EDGE.

Serves 4   Preparation time 10 minutes   Cooking time 15–20 minutes

1 cup quinoa
1 cup cooked basmati rice
1 small bag watercress
1 small bag arugula
³/₄ cup salted honeyed cashews, chopped
salt and freshly ground black pepper

DRESSING
5 tablespoons olive oil
juice of 2 large limes
juice of 1 orange
1 garlic clove, crushed
1 large red onion, finely sliced

✱ Put the quinoa into a saucepan and cover well with cold water. Bring to a boil, then reduce the heat and simmer gently for about 15 minutes, or until just tender but nice and nutty; do not overcook. Strain well and transfer to a bowl, then add the cooked rice and mix well.

✱ For the dressing, combine the olive oil and lime and orange juices in a separate bowl, then add the garlic and sliced onion and mix well.

✱ Roughly chop the watercress and arugula, then add to the quinoa and rice along with the cashews.

✱ Add the dressing, season well with salt and pepper, and mix well. Serve with the Juicy Pork Chops with Strawberries & Mustard (see opposite).

Grilled pork chops with baked pears

BRINING IS NOTHING NEW. IN FACT, IT'S BEEN AROUND FOR CENTURIES—TAKE DELICIOUS BACON, FOR EXAMPLE. THE SECRET OF SUCCESS IS TO BRINE ONLY LIGHTLY, AS WITH THESE CHOPS, WHICH REQUIRE 20 MINUTES MAXIMUM—YES, JUST 20 MINUTES. AS THEY SAY, JUST TASTE THE DIFFERENCE...

Serves 4   Preparation time 20 minutes   Cooking time 2 hours

PEARS
4 large ripe Bosc pears
$^1/_2$ cup maple syrup
$^1/_2$ cup olive oil
salt and freshly ground black pepper

BRINE
2 tablespoons sugar
1 tablespoons salt
$1^1/_4$ cups water

4 thick and fatty bone-in pork chops, about 1in thick
2 tablespoons olive oil

✱ Preheat the oven to 375°F.

✱ Cut the pears in half lengthwise, then cut a small sliver off the bottom of each so they sit nicely level. Scoop out the core and seeds with a spoon. Put the pears on a baking sheet.

✱ Drizzle with the maple syrup and olive oil and season with a touch of salt and pepper. Bake for about 2 hours, or until soft. The pears will shrivel and brown slightly, but the flavor will intensify by about threefold.

✱ Meanwhile, put the brine ingredients into a stainless steel saucepan. Dissolve the sugar and salt slowly into the water over low heat, then bring to a boil. Remove from the heat and let cool, then add enough cold water to match the original quantity of brine (1½ cups).

✱ Pour half the brine into a small glass, ceramic, or stainless steel dish. Place the chops in the dish so that they fit nice and tightly. Pour in the remainder of the brine. Cover and let stand at room temperature for 20 minutes, no more.

✱ When you are ready to cook, remove the chops from the brine and pat dry with paper towels. Heat the olive oil in a frying pan. Lightly pepper the chops, then cook gently for 4–5 minutes on each side until cooked through.

✱ Arrange the baked pears, roughly sliced, topping the chops. Serve with some lightly cooked green beans.

Cider-roasted pork belly with apples & celery

YOU REALLY CAN'T GO WRONG WITH ANY DISH THAT MATCHES CIDER WITH PORK. IT IS SUCH A CLASSIC COMBINATION IN COOKING, AND ONE THAT HARKENS BACK TO THE CUSTOM MANY YEARS AGO FOR PIGS TO BE LET OUT TO GORGE ON THE FALLEN APPLES IN ORDER TO CLEAR THE ORCHARDS. BELLY IS PERFECT FOR THIS SORT OF COOKING—NOT TOO FATTY, AND THIN ENOUGH TO ROAST QUICKLY AND EVENLY. ROASTING IN A SMALL AMOUNT OF LIQUID IN AN ENCLOSED PAN IS IDEAL. YOU WILL BE AMAZED HOW MUCH STOCK THERE WILL BE AT THE END, MAKING A GREAT SAUCE/COMPOTE.

Serves 4   Preparation time 30 minutes   Cooking time about 2 hours in total, probably less

1¹/₂lb piece of boneless, rindless pork belly
salt and freshly ground black pepper
2 tablespoons oil (any type will do)
3¹/₂oz chorizo or any spicy sausage, roughly chopped (optional)
4 large celery ribs, finely chopped
2 large onions, very finely chopped
1 large Macintosh apple, peeled, cored, and finely chopped
6 garlic cloves, finely chopped
a few fresh sage leaves
³/₄ cup dry cider
³/₄ cup well-flavored pork or chicken stock

✱ Preheat the oven to 350°F.

✱ Season the pork belly well with salt and pepper. Heat the oil in a deep, ovenproof pan with a tight-fitting lid on the stove, add the chorizo, if using, and cook until the fat starts to run.

✱ Add the pork belly and brown well on both sides, then carefully remove from the pan, leaving the chorizo.

✱ Add the vegetables, apple, garlic, and sage to the pan and top with the pork, then pour in the cider and stock. Bring to a boil and cover with the lid.

✱ Cook in the oven for 1 hour and 30–45 minutes, or until the pork is soft and well cooked—but do not overcook!

✱ Remove the pork from the pan and carefully chop or slice. Gently mash the vegetables and apples with the gravy and juices in the pan and cook on the stove until thickened slightly. Serve with the pork.

Roast pork loin with crackling & applesauce

THERE ARE TWO KEY ISSUES HERE: ONE, SCORE THE RIND AND FAT REALLY WELL, AS THIS WILL ENSURE THAT THE FAT WILL BE RELEASED, MAKING A CRISPER CRACKLING; TWO, DO NOT OVERCOOK AND BE CERTAIN TO REST THE PORK, WELL WRAPPED IN FOIL. I ALWAYS SAY TO REST MEAT FOR AS LONG AS YOU COOK IT. YES, THAT'S AN HOUR IN THIS CASE, BUT IT WILL BE FINE, TRUST ME—JUST POP IT BACK IN THE OVEN TO WARM UP AGAIN.

Serves 6-8   Preparation time 15 minutes   Cooking time 1 hour 15-45 minutes

3¼lb boneless rolled pork loin, rind scored with a knife
salt and freshly ground black pepper
1 tablespoon all-purpose flour
1¼ cups hot chicken or pork stock

APPLESAUCE
½ teaspoon ground allspice
about ¾ cup cold water
3 large, tart cooking apples, such as Macintoshs, peeled, cored, and chopped
3½ tablespoons unsalted butter

✻ Preheat the oven to 375°F.

✻ Rip off about a 20in length of foil from the roll and scrunch up into a small bed for the pork to sit on—this is to keep the bottom of the pork from cooking in its own fat and juices—and place in a roasting pan. Season the pork rind well with salt and pepper, sit the pork on the scrunched-up foil, and pop the pork in the oven. Roast for 1 hour.

✻ For the applesauce, put the spice, water, and apples in a saucepan, cover with a lid, and cook for 15 minutes until the apples are soft and pulpy and you have a nice thick stew. Season with a little salt and pepper and stir in the butter. Keep warm.

✻ After 1 hour, remove the pork from the oven and check that it is cooked by inserting a skewer or thin-bladed knife into the thickest part of the meat—the juices should run clear. If not, return to the oven for another 15-30 minutes.

✻ Remove the pork rind with a long-bladed knife, ensuring that you keep most of the fat on the loin. Place the rind on a baking sheet, fat-side up, and pop back in the oven for about 15-20 minutes to crisp up further, but watch closely as the crackling will quickly burn.

✻ Meanwhile, wrap the pork well in foil and let rest in a warm place to let the juices settle and the meat tenderize.

✻ Place the roasting pan on the stove and scrape off all the pieces stuck to the bottom. Mix the flour with a little water in a cup. Spoon off a little of the fat, then add the flour and water mixture and stir well to soak up the remaining fat. Blend in the hot stock and cook, stirring well, until thickened, then pour into a bowl and keep warm.

✻ Cut the pork into thick slices and serve topped with pieces of the crisp crackling and the warm applesauce on the side.

Pork tenderloin scallops with blackcurrants & heavy cream

THE TANGY EDGE OF BLACKCURRANTS REALLY HELPS BRING OUT THE FLAVOR OF PORK AND CREAM. IF FRESH BLACKCURRANTS AREN'T READILY AVAILBLE, TRY USING CANNED BLACKCURRANTS OR EVEN BLUEBERRIES AS A DELICIOUS SUBSTITUTE.

Serves 4   Preparation time 30 minutes, plus chilling   Cooking time 25 minutes

1 pork tenderloin, about 1lb 2oz,
   without fat or silver sinew
3 eggs
1 tablespoon milk
5 tablespoons vegetable oil
1/4 cup all-purpose flour
6 tablespoons dried bread crumbs
6 tablespoons cornmeal (fine polenta)
1 small onion, finely chopped
1 garlic clove, crushed
3/4 cup dry white wine
1 1/4 cups good-quality chicken stock
3 1/2 oz fresh blackcurrants (frozen are also fine,
   or use canned)
2/3 cup heavy cream
salt and freshly ground black pepper
squeeze of lemon juice

✱ Place the pork on a cutting board and cut into four pieces, then cut each piece of pork three-quarters of the way through lengthwise and open out flat.

✱ Lay a large piece of plastic wrap over a cutting board. Place one piece of pork on the plastic wrap, add ½ teaspoon water, and fold the plastic wrap over the top. Using a rolling pin or meat mallet, gently beat the pork nice and thin, the thinner the better. (The water helps the pork to move inside the plastic wrap.) Repeat the process with the other three pieces of pork.

✱ Put the eggs, milk, and 1 tablespoon vegetable oil into a bowl and beat together well. Put the flour into one dish and combine the bread crumbs and cornmeal in another. Dust the pork lightly with flour, then dip, one at a time, into the egg mixture then into the bread crumbs and cornmeal. Chill well.

✱ Meanwhile, place the onion and garlic in a saucepan, add the white wine, and bring to a boil. Reduce the heat and simmer until about 1 tablespoon remains.

✱ Add the stock and cook down until you have about half the original volume. Add the blackcurrants (if fresh) and cook for 3–4 minutes. (If using frozen fruit, pop them in straight from the freezer and cook for 5–6 minutes.)

✱ Add the cream and bring to a boil, but do not reduce. Season well with salt and pepper and taste, adjusting with a little sugar if needed and a squeeze of lemon juice. If you are using canned blackcurrants, add them now so that the residual heat warms them through, then cover.

✱ Heat the remaining vegetable oil in a frying pan, add two pork scallops, and cook quickly in the hot oil until slightly browned on the bottom. Turn over and cook for another 3–4 minutes. Remove from the pan, drain well, and keep warm while you repeat the process with the remaining scallops.

✱ To serve, spoon a little sauce onto each warmed plate and top with a hot pork scallop. Serve the extra sauce separately. All you will need with it is a crisp green salad and a few new potatoes rolled in minted butter.

Bonfire spiced pork & prune patties

THIS IS A QUICK AND EASY DISH TO MAKE, AND ADDING PRUNES TO THE PORK REALLY SWEETENS THE MEAT NICELY. I LIKE TO COOK THESE PATTIES ON AN OPEN FIRE.

Serves 4   Preparation time 20 minutes   Cooking time about 10 minutes

SAUCE
1 cup ketchup
$\frac{1}{2}$ cup cold water
2 tablespoons Worcestershire sauce
$\frac{1}{4}$ cup light brown sugar
1 tablespoon honey
3 tablespoons malt vinegar
2 teaspoons English mustard powder
1 teaspoon Cajun seasoning
1 teaspoon ground cumin
2 pinches of chopped fresh chile
salt and freshly ground black pepper

6 ready-to-eat pitted prunes
1lb lean ground pork
2 tablespoons chopped fresh sage
$\frac{1}{4}$ teaspoon ground nutmeg
2 pinches of chile powder
1 tablespoon mayonnaise
1 egg, lightly beaten
2 tablespoons vegetable oil

✱ Put all the sauce ingredients into a saucepan and bring to a boil. Reduce the heat and simmer gently for 2 minutes, or until slightly thickened. Season with salt and pepper. Keep hot or let cool, ready for serving.

✱ Chop the prunes into small pieces and put in a bowl. Add the ground pork, sage, nutmeg, chile powder, and mayonnaise and season really well with salt and pepper. Then mix in a little of the beaten egg to bind everything together.

✱ Mold the mixture into eight small flat patties. Alternatively, you can mold the mixture onto small bamboo skewers, presoaked in cold water for 30 minutes. They can be cooked in the same way as the patties.

✱ Heat the oil in a large non-stick frying pan and cook the patties (or skewers) on each side for about 4–5 minutes. Serve immediately with the hot or cooled sauce.

Velveted pork tenderloin with peppers & garlic

PORK TENDERLOIN, I HAVE FOUND, CAN COOK UP RATHER BLAND, DRY, AND TASTELESS. MY GOOD FRIEND KEN HOM SHOWED ME THIS TRICK MANY YEARS AGO, SO THANKS KEN! VELVETING IS A SIMPLE PROCESS IN WHICH YOU COAT MEAT OR FISH IN A MIXTURE OF BEATEN EGG WHITE, A LITTLE OIL, A PINCH OF SALT, AND CORNSTARCH. THIS MIXTURE THEN CLINGS TO THE MEAT OR FISH AND, ONCE COOKED, SEALS IN ANY MOISTURE, MAKING THE FINISHED DISH BEAUTIFULLY TENDER AND MOIST.

Serves 4   Preparation time 10 minutes   Cooking time 15 minutes

1 egg white
1 tablespoon cornstarch
1 pork tenderloin, about 1lb 2oz, without fat or silver sinew, cut into 8–12 slices
1 red bell pepper, seeded and cut into strips
1 yellow bell pepper, seeded and cut into strips
1 onion, very finely sliced
salt
4 tablespoons vegetable oil
2 garlic cloves, finely chopped
8 scallions, or 1 small bunch, finely sliced
6 tablespoons dark soy sauce

✱ Put the egg white and cornstarch in a bowl with a pinch of salt, whisk together briefly, then fold through the pork slices until evenly coated.

✱ Put the bell peppers and onion in a saucepan with a pinch of salt, cover with water, bring to a boil, then immediately drain and let cool.

✱ Heat a wok or non-stick frying pan with 2 tablespoons of the vegetable oil. Add half the pork slices and stir-fry until nicely colored, then remove from the pan to a plate. Repeat with the remaining pork until it is all sealed and then keep warm.

✱ Wipe out the pan with paper towels and reheat with the remaining 2 tablespoons oil. Add the cooled peppers and onion, garlic, and scallions and stir-fry over high heat for 3–4 minutes, or until softened and colored.

✱ Return the pork to the pan, add the soy sauce, and stir well. Then, stir in any pork juice left over on the plate before serving with boiled or steamed plain rice or rice noodles.

Pork tenderloin with black peppercorns, vinegar & yellow bean sauce

THIS IS A GREAT WAY TO EAT PORK TENDERLOIN, BUT BE CAREFUL NOT TO OVERCOOK IT, OR THE MEAT WILL BE DRY AND TOUGH. I HAVE NO PROBLEM USING A STORE-BOUGHT SAUCE, AVAILABLE IN GOURMET SUPERMARKETS OR ONLINE, ESPECIALLY BECAUSE SOME OF THEM ARE OF SUCH GOOD QUALITY.

Serves 4   Preparation time 10 minutes   Cooking time 25 minutes

1 pork tenderloin, about 1lb 2oz, without fat and silver sinew, cut into 8 slices
2 tablespoons olive oil
2 tablespoons unsalted butter
salt
2 tablespoons all-purpose flour
1 teaspoon lightly crushed black peppercorns
2 tablespoons white wine vinegar
3 tablespoons good-quality Chinese yellow bean sauce
$3/4$ cup heavy cream
6 tablespoons roughly chopped fresh flat-leaf parsley
sugar, to taste

✻ Flatten each slice of pork tenderloin with the blade of a knife so that you end up with eight small scallops.

✻ Heat the olive oil and butter in a non-stick frying pan. Season the scallops with a little salt, then gently dust with flour, shaking off the excess. Place four scallops into the hot oil and melted butter and cook over medium heat for 3–4 minutes each side—they should be nicely browned and golden. Remove from the pan and keep warm, then repeat with the remaining scallops.

✻ Add the crushed peppercorns and vinegar and swirl around the pan—the vinegar will mostly evaporate—then add the yellow bean sauce and heat through. Stir in the cream and bring to a boil, then add the parsley. Season with a little sugar, and salt if needed.

✻ Return all the pork to the pan, spoon over the sauce, and serve with boiled or steamed plain rice.

Pumpkin & pork hot pot

THE TRADITIONAL WAY OF MAKING HOT POT IS TO CASSEROLE LAMB NECK WITH A POTATO CRUST PACKED FULL OF ROOT VEGETABLES. IN THIS VERSION I HAVE ADDED BLOOD SAUSAGE AND PUMPKIN, THE LATTER REPLACING THE USUAL RUTABAGA AND TURNIP AND THE FORMER GIVING THE WHOLE DISH A PEPPERY BITE, AND HAVE USED PORK NECK CHOPS INSTEAD OF LAMB, AS THEY HAVE A LITTLE MORE MEAT ON THEM AND SLIGHTLY LESS FAT, BUT YOU CAN USE THICK-CUT PORK CHOPS TOO. YOU CAN ALSO ADD SOAKED PEARL BARLEY IF YOU WISH FOR AN ADDED LAYER OF TEXTURE.

Serves 4   Preparation time 20 minutes   Cooking time about 2 hours

4–6 tablespoons vegetable oil
1 large carrot, peeled and chopped
2 small onions, roughly chopped
2 large garlic cloves, crushed
4 pork neck chops or thick pork chops
10oz peeled and seeded pumpkin, diced
salt and freshly ground black pepper
4oz good-quality blood sausage, sliced on the diagonal
1 beef bouillon cube, dissolved in about 2^1/$_2$ cups boiling water
2 tablespoons all-purpose flour
4 large baking potatoes, peeled and not-too-thinly sliced
melted butter, for brushing

✱ Preheat the oven to 350°F.

✱ Heat half the oil in a sauté pan and cook the carrot, onions, and garlic together until they have wilted and taken on a nice color.

✱ Heat the remaining oil in a frying pan and cook the chops until nicely browned on both sides, then transfer to a roasting pan or ovenproof dish with a tight-fitting lid.

✱ Spread the pumpkin and the cooked vegetable mixture over the chops and season well with salt and pepper, then top with the sausage slices.

✱ Blend the warm stock into the flour, then pour over the chops to just cover them. Carefully top with the sliced potatoes, season well with salt and pepper, and brush with melted butter.

✱ Cover with foil or the lid and cook in the oven for about 1 hour. Remove the foil and return the pan or dish to the oven for another 45 minutes–1 hour to brown up the potatoes. You may need to increase the oven temperature to crisp them up.

✱ This dish is best cooked and eaten when it has been left to cool for about 30 minutes. I'm a big fan of pickled cabbage and it works perfectly with a hot pot, so just dive in.

My Pho

HAVING BEEN TO VIETNAM RECENTLY, IT MADE SENSE TO INCLUDE MY VERSION OF THE COUNTRY'S NATIONAL DISH, *PHO*, PRONOUNCED "FIR" IN VIETNAMESE. I HAD A BEEF PHO FOR BREAKFAST, EATEN ON THE SIDE OF THE STREET VERY EARLY ONE MORNING. THE FRESHNESS OF THE DISH REALLY MADE AN IMPACT ON ME, WITH ITS TASTY, CLEAN FLAVORS ALL WORKING WELL TOGETHER. IT IS ALSO GLUTEN FREE, SOMETHING THAT IS CLOSE TO MY HEART. THERE ARE MANY VARIATIONS OF PHO TO BE FOUND IN VIETNAM FROM NORTH TO SOUTH, USING CHICKEN OR FISH AS WELL AS BEEF. ONE IS EVEN SERVED WITH SLICED BREAD FOR DUNKING.

Serves 4   Preparation time 20 minutes   Cooking time 15 minutes

1 quart good-quality chicken or pork stock or use 1 quart water and
   3–4 chicken or pork bouillon cubes, crumbled
8 scallions, sliced on the diagonal
1 small fresh red chile, finely chopped
2 garlic cloves, crushed
2 tablespoons Vietnamese fish sauce (*nuoc cham*)
1 tablespoon palm sugar or granulated sugar
salt and freshly ground black pepper
1 small pork tenderloin, about ³⁄₄lb, without fat or silver sinew
7oz cooked rice vermicelli or other fine rice noodles
1¹⁄₂ cups bean sprouts
1 small bunch fresh cilantro
1 small bunch fresh Thai basil or any other basil
10 fresh mint leaves
juice of 2 large limes

✱ Put the stock or water and bouillon cubes into a large saucepan and heat until just simmering.

✱ Add the scallions, chile, garlic, fish sauce, sugar, and a little salt and pepper.

✱ Meanwhile, cut the pork into very thin slices across the loin, then into four.

✱ Add the pork to the stock and stir well—it will cook almost immediately.

✱ Add the noodles and bean sprouts, return to a simmer, and then turn off the heat.

✱ Roughly chop the herbs and add to the pan along with the lime juice. Serve immediately. You can serve a little soy sauce with the pho if you want, along with extra limes for squeezing, herbs, and even more chile.

Pork jalfrezi

CHICKEN IS THE NORM FOR JALFREZI, WHICH ORIGINATED AS A USE-UP DISH IN THE DAYS OF THE RAJ. THE WELL-TO-DO FAMILIES IN DELHI ALWAYS HAD A ROAST ON A SUNDAY, AND ANY LEFTOVER ROASTED MEAT WAS REUSED ON MONDAY IN A SORT OF STIR-FRY. I ENJOYED A PARTICULARLY DELICIOUS JALFREZI COOKED BY THE CHEF OF THE OBEROI HOTEL IN NEW DELHI, SO HERE IS THE PRODUCT OF WHAT I LEARNED FROM THAT EXPERIENCE.

Serves 4   Preparation time 30 minutes   Cooking time 15 minutes

1 x 14oz can chopped tomatoes in juice
$1/2$ vegetable bouillon cube, crumbled
1 tablespoon tomato paste
4 tablespoons vegetable oil
2 small pork tenderloins, $10^{1}/_{2}$–12oz each, or 1 large, about 1lb 2oz,
   without fat and silver sinew, cut into 12 pieces
1 tablespoon very finely chopped fresh ginger
1 garlic clove, finely chopped
1–2 teaspoons roughly chopped fresh red chile
1 teaspoon ground cumin
1 teaspoon ground coriander
$1/2$ teaspoon ground turmeric
1 small onion, very finely chopped
1 small red bell pepper, seeded and sliced
1 small yellow bell pepper, seeded and sliced
1 small green bell pepper, seeded and sliced
sugar, to taste
salt and freshly ground black pepper
2 tablespoons chopped fresh cilantro

* Put the tomatoes, bouillon cube, and tomato paste in a saucepan and cook down until you have a thick stew.

* Heat half the oil in a large pan, add the pork pieces, and cook for 6–8 minutes until well browned and cooked through; do not overcook. Remove from the saucepan and keep warm.

* Heat the remaining oil in the pan, add the ginger and garlic, and cook for a couple of minutes. Add the chile, cumin, coriander, and turmeric and lightly cook.

* Add the onion and peppers and stir-fry until slightly wilted. Add the tomato mixture and pork and stir to coat— you may need to add a touch of water. The sauce should coat the vegetable and meat well, like a dry stir-fry. Season with a little sugar and salt and pepper, and add the fresh cilantro.

* Serve with boiled or steamed rice and naan bread.

My pork tikka masala

PURISTS WILL POUR SCORN ON THIS RECIPE, BUT IT HAS A GREAT STORY TO IT. REZZA, MY GOOD INDIAN FRIEND AND WONDERFUL CHEF, AND I WERE COOKING IN GLASGOW AT THE SHISH MAHAL, THE RESTAURANT WHERE CHICKEN TIKKA MASALA WAS INVENTED. ASIF, THE SON OF THE ORIGINAL OWNER, TOLD ME THAT IN THE EARLY 1970S, A BUS DRIVER CAME INTO THE RESTAURANT LATE ONE EVENING. HE ORDERED CHICKEN TIKKA, BUT AFTER A FEW MINUTES SENT IT BACK TO THE KITCHEN SAYING IT WAS DRY. ASIF'S FATHER, RECOVERING FROM AN ULCER AT THE TIME, WAS EATING CANNED SOUP. HE TOLD THE CHEF TO ADD THE CANNED SOUP TO THE TIKKA AND WARM IT THROUGH. THE BUS DRIVER LOVED IT AND THE CHICKEN TIKKA MASALA WAS BORN. TO THIS DAY THE RESTAURANT STILL SERVES THE DISH (BUT NOT WITH CANNED SOUP), AND THEY SELL 25,000 PORTIONS A YEAR. I HAVE RECREATED THE ORIGINAL RECIPE, COMPLETE WITH CANNED SOUP. WHAT FUN!

Serves 4   Preparation time 40 minutes, plus overnight marinating   Cooking time about 45 minutes

MARINADE

1 tablespoon very finely grated fresh ginger
3 garlic cloves, very finely crushed
2 tablespoons ground coriander
1 tablespoon smoked paprika
2 teaspoons garam masala
1 teaspoon ground cumin
1/2 teaspoon red chile powder
2 tablespoons oil (any type will do)
1/2 cup thick Greek yogurt

2 pork tenderloins, about 3/4lb each, without fat and silver sinew, cut into 1 1/2in pieces
salt and freshly ground black pepper

SAUCE

1/4 cup oil
2 tablespoons ground coriander
4 teaspoons paprika
2 teaspoons ground turmeric
2 teaspoons garam masala
2 teaspoons fenugreek leaves
1/2 teaspoon ground cloves
1/4 cup grated fresh ginger
1 small red chile, very finely chopped
2 large onions, very finely chopped
4 garlic cloves, finely chopped
4 ripe tomatoes, chopped
1 x 14oz can condensed tomato soup
1 chicken bouillon cube, crumbled
1/2 cup heavy cream
sugar, to taste
3–5 tablespoons cold unsalted butter, cut into cubes
a few fresh cilantro leaves

✱ Put all the marinade ingredients into a glass or ceramic bowl and mix really well. Add the pork pieces and mix well again, adding a little salt and pepper. Cover and leave to marinate in the fridge overnight.

✱ For the sauce, heat the oil in a large pan, add the ground coriander, paprika, turmeric, garam masala, fenugreek, cloves, ginger, and chile, and cook for a minute or two. Add the onions and garlic and cook again for a few minutes.

✱ Next, add the tomatoes, soup, bouillon cube, cream, and a little water and cook for 15–20 minutes, or until the onions are cooked and the sauce is slightly reduced.

✱ Meanwhile, preheat a broiler to its hottest setting. Blend the sauce in a blender until really smooth, then pour back into the saucepan and bring to a simmer.

✱ Remove the pork from the fridge, place the chunks on a baking sheet and broil for 3–4 minutes on each side until half cooked. Place straight into the simmering sauce and simmer for 4–5 minutes to finish cooking; do not overcook. Season well with salt and pepper and add sugar to balance.

✱ Finally, add the butter and shake the pan until the sauce is thickened and glossy. Add the fresh cilantro and serve.

Pork & shrimp spring rolls with dipping sauce

SPRING ROLLS ARE EATEN EVERYWHERE IN THE MEKONG DELTA IN SOUTHERN VIETNAM, FILLED WITH MANY VARIETIES OF FISH, HERBS, AND VEGETABLES. DURING MY RECENT VISIT TO THE COUNTRY, I ENJOYED A SUPERB EXAMPLE OF THEM IN A TINY RESTAURANT THAT PREPARED THE FISH TO ORDER, FRESH AS A DAISY. SO WITH THAT IN MIND, HERE IS MY VERSION FOR A SNACK OR MAIN COURSE DISH THAT IS DELICIOUS AND VERY EASY TO MAKE AND SERVE, ALONG WITH A LITTLE SWEET AND SOUR DIPPING SAUCE.

Serves 4   Preparation time 20 minutes   Cooking time 15–20 minutes

FILLING

4 large shrimp, peeled
1 small pork tenderloin, about 10½–12oz,
  without fat or silver sinew
1 teaspoon very finely chopped fresh red chile
2 teaspoons Vietnamese fish sauce (*nuoc cham*)
2 heaping teaspoons shrimp paste (optional)
2 garlic cloves, crushed
salt and freshly ground black pepper

1 carrot, peeled
4 scallions
½ small cucumber

DIPPING SAUCE

¼ cup soy sauce
1 tablespoon Vietnamese fish sauce (*nuoc cham*)
1 small red chile, finely chopped
2 tablespoons chopped fresh cilantro
1 tablespoon palm sugar or granulated sugar

16 spring roll wrappers
1 small bunch fresh Thai basil or any other basil
a few fresh mint leaves
1 small bunch fresh cilantro
vegetable oil, for deep-frying

✱ For the filling, chop the shrimp and also the pork tenderloin, the finer the better—if you have a grinder you can use here, then great.

✱ Put the shrimp and pork in a bowl, add the chile, fish sauce, shrimp paste, if using, garlic, and salt and pepper, and mix really well.

✱ Next, finely slice the vegetables into thin strips, the thinner the better—matchstick size is about right.

✱ Put all the ingredients for the dipping sauce in a small bowl and mix well.

✱ Lightly wet one side of a spring roll wrapper with a pastry brush or your fingers. Place a small sausage of the shrimp and pork mixture on the wrapper to one side. Top with a few carrot, scallion, and cucumber matchsticks, then add a few leaves of each herb.

✱ Fold the sides of the wrapper into the center and then roll up, making sure that the top lip is wetted again, and seal well. Repeat the process with the remaining wrappers.

✱ Heat 1in of vegetable oil in a wok or deep frying pan to about 325°F. Cook the spring rolls in batches of no more than four for about 3–4 minutes, turning once, until crispy and cooked through.

✱ Serve the spring rolls hot with the dipping sauce.

CHAPTER 3 Ham

Ham, like bacon, is a cured product that is eaten extensively all over the globe, from the world-famous dry-cured hams such as prosciutto and jamòn Ibérico to the well-known cooked hams like Smithfield or Virginia ham. The word ham generally refers to a cured leg of pork that is ready to eat, whether it is cooked or dry cured. Fresh hams are usually brined and roasted.

My particular enthusiasm is for producing dry-cured hams that need no cooking after the production process has finished. Many people in the UK have tried to reproduce the flavor of Parma and Ibérico, and failed miserably. With this in mind, I set about trying to produce a British dry-cured ham using continental methods as guidelines, and I have to say that after ten years of tortuous experimentation I have a product that would stand up against any of the more well-known hams and that won a major accolade in the UK's leading food award scheme in 2009, the Great Taste Awards.

Cooked hams also remain popular in the modern deli and butcher's shop, although I have to say that the products generally available could only be loosely described as ham. I have seen ham commercially produced where brine is injected into legs of pork at levels of up to 45 percent and, with the use of functional ingredients such as phosphates, soy protein, and carrageenan, will produce cooking yields of up to 120 percent, which means the finished ham will be 20 percent heavier than the leg you started with! This, unfortunately, is what happens when supermarkets rule the world with the overwhelming desire to sell the cheapest food.

Selecting the meat

WHETHER PRODUCING EITHER DRY-CURED OR COOKED HAM, MY MEAT SELECTION PROCESS IS THE SAME:

✱ I use legs from female pigs only that weigh 175–220lb dead weight. Male pigs in the UK are not castrated as a rule and the meat from such animals contains the sex hormones androstenone, testosterone and skatole, which can give an unpleasant flavor to the meat. However, in the US, male pigs are castrated by law so you could use either male or female.

✱ The legs should exhibit pH values of 5.5–5.8 or be three days post-slaughter.

✱ I always break the leg down into its different muscles for curing. This helps reduce curing times, and I also prefer the texture of single-muscle products.

CHOOSING A LEG ALSO ENABLES YOU TO PRODUCE MORE THAN ONE KIND OF HAM, AS THE LEG CONSISTS OF FOUR MAJOR MUSCLES:

1 Inside muscle I use this muscle for a cooked ham, as it is lean and tender once cured and cooked.

2 Outside muscle This is the one I use for a dry-cured ham. It's probably the toughest muscle in the leg, but the dry-curing process and lengthy maturation time, along with enzymatic activity, results in a product that melts in the mouth once cured.

3 Knuckle This muscle makes a wonderful little cooked ham, especially when flavored with asparagus.

4 Rump My favorite part of the leg, this makes the most delightful dry-cured ham, especially when lightly smoked over beechwood.

✱ The trimmings can be used for sausages.

DRY*-CURED
HAMS
*(AIR)

COPPA ⟫⟫⟶

LOMO ⟫⟫⟶

Brickhill ham

USE EITHER OUTSIDE MUSCLE OR RUMP FOR THIS METHOD. IN A COLD, DAMP CLIMATE, YOU MAY SEE MOLD GROWING ON YOUR HAM. THIS WILL NOT AFFECT THE QUALITY OF YOUR HAM AND YOU CAN REMOVE IT BY WIPING THE OUTSIDE OF THE HAM WITH A CLOTH SOAKED IN VINEGAR (WHITE DISTILLED VINEGAR IS FINE).

YOU WILL NEED PER 2¼LB PORK:

2 tablespoons + 1 teaspoon curing salt (containing 1% sodium nitrite and 0.8% potassium nitrate)
¾ teaspoon dextrose (the heaviest of the sugars, which helps counteract the toughening effect of the salt)
½ teaspoon sodium ascorbate (the sodium salt of ascorbic acid, which helps to stabilize the cure color)
spices/herbs (optional)—black peppercorns, coriander seeds, or garlic powder can be added,
   but if you have a nice enough piece of meat to start with, there is no need to flavor it
fibrous casing (man-made casing derived from collagen), for wrapping the ham

✱ Mix all the curing ingredients together thoroughly and apply half the mixture to the meat, paying special attention to the thicker parts.

✱ Place in a suitably sized, robust plastic food container and leave to cure for 7 days in a cold fridge at a temperature of 34–38°F, making sure the meat is turned over at least once. During this time a brine will form in the bottom of the container, which should be discarded at regular intervals.

✱ After 7 days, apply the rest of the cure mix as before and leave to cure for another 2 weeks, ensuring that you turn the meat every 2 days.

✱ After the 2 weeks, wash the ham off in lukewarm water and let dry in a cool, airy place for a couple of hours.

✱ Once dry, the ham can be wrapped in the casing/bung and left to "equalize" or "burn through" for another week in the fridge—this process allows the salt and other additives to diffuse through to the center of the ham.

✱ The last step is to hang the ham somewhere cool with little air flow—a cellar or pantry would be ideal—to mature and dry. The ham should be ready to eat when it is quite firm to the touch but not rock hard, 8–12 weeks.

Coppa

This is an Italian speciality made from the shoulder or neck of the pig. I actually prefer this to dry-cured ham because it contains a bit more fat and is somewhat sweeter in taste. It was with this product that I won a three-star gold award at the Great Taste Awards in 2009. The curing ingredients and method are the same as for dry-cured ham, but you will find that it will be ready a little sooner than the ham—probably in 6–8 weeks.

Lomo

This Spanish delicacy is made from the eye of the loin. Again, the recipe is the same as for dry-cured ham, but adding ¾ tablespoon smoked paprika to the cure mix will give it authenticity.

SMOKED HAMS

Kassler

THIS IS A GERMAN SPECIALITY THAT, SADLY, IS NOT AS POPULAR AS IT SHOULD BE. WHEN MADE CORRECTLY IT IS ABSOLUTELY DELICIOUS, WHETHER HOT OR COLD.

YOU WILL NEED PER 2¼LB BONELESS, RINDLESS LOIN:

2 cups water
2³/₄ tablespoons curing salt (containing 0.6% sodium nitrite and 0.8% potassium nitrate)
½ teaspoon dextrose
¼ teaspoon sodium ascorbate

✱ Mix the brine ingredients together thoroughly in a large, deep, strong plastic or stainless steel bowl or container—the easiest way is to use warm water and then chill the brine, but you can use cold water if you prefer.

✱ Immerse the loin in the brine so that it is completely covered. Leave in the fridge for a week.

✱ Remove the ham from the brine and leave in a cool, airy place for another 2 days until it is dry to the touch.

✱ Apply a light smoke (see page 107), setting the smoker for indirect cooking at a temperature of 172°F and cooking until a core of 155°F is reached.

Westphalian-style ham

A TRUE WESTPHALIAN HAM IS A TOP-QUALITY AIR-DRIED SMOKED HAM FROM GERMANY. IN MY VERSION, I USE THE SAME CURING METHOD AS FOR THE BRICKHILL HAM (SEE PAGE 81). I USUALLY SMOKE THE HAM FOR ABOUT 30 MINUTES AND THEN, INSTEAD OF THE LENGTHY DRYING PERIOD, STEAM COOK AT A TEMPERATURE OF 172°F UNTIL A CORE TEMPERATURE OF 155°F IS REACHED.

COOKED HAMS

Brine curing

USE INSIDE MUSCLE, TOP RUMP, OR HAM HOCK. YOU WILL NEED A QUANTITY OF BRINE APPROXIMATELY HALF THE WEIGHT OF THE HAM, AS FOLLOWS:

YOU WILL NEED PER 2¼LB PORK:

1¼ cups water
¼ cup curing salt (containing 0.6% sodium nitrite and 0.8% potassium nitrate)
5 teaspoons sodium ascorbate
½ cup ice

✱ Mix the brine ingredients together thoroughly in a large, deep strong plastic or stainless steel bowl or container—the easiest way is to use warm water and mix in the curing salt and sodium ascorbate, then add the ice.

✱ Take your selected muscle and ensure that it is trimmed of all visible gristle and sinew. Immerse the ham in the brine so that it is completely covered. Leave in the fridge for a week.

✱ Remove the ham from the brine and let dry off in a cool, airy place for another 2 days before cooking. Phil's recipe for Baked Brown Sugar Glazed Ham Hocks with Cloves, Tamarind, and English Mustard (see page 86) is my particular favorite.

Asparagus ham

You will need the same ingredients for the brine as above but with the addition of ¼oz asparagus flavoring (a totally natural brine additive available from good butchers) per 2¼lb meat.

Burgundy ham

Again, the recipe is the same as above but with the addition of ¼oz burgundy flavoring (a totally natural brine additive available from good butchers) to the brine per 2¼lb meat.

Baked brown sugar glazed ham hocks with cloves, tamarind & English mustard

I COOKED THIS ON A TV SPECIAL SOME YEARS AGO AND IT'S BEEN A CHRISTMAS FAVORITE EVER SINCE. THE SKIN AND FAT TAKE ON A REALLY POWERFUL FLAVOR, AND THEY LOOK STUNNING.

Serves 6–8   Preparation time 20 minutes, plus overnight soaking, then chilling   Cooking time about 3 hours in total

4 brined ham hocks (see page 85)
salt (optional)
2 carrots, peeled but left whole
2 celery ribs
$1/2$ leek, washed well but left whole
2 onions, peeled but left whole
2 tablespoons black peppercorns
4 bay leaves
1 head of garlic

GLAZE
2 cups dark brown sugar
$1^{1}/_{2}$ cups dry cider
$1/4$ cup tamarind paste
$1/4$ cup olive oil
$1/3$ cup honey
2 tablespoons English mustard/ English mustard powder
1 tablespoon smoked paprika
1 teaspoon ground cloves

✱ Soak the hocks in cold water overnight.

✱ Drain the hocks and wash them really well, then place in a deep pan. Fill with cold water and bring to a boil. Reduce the heat and simmer for 5 minutes, then taste the water: if it's salty, pour a little out and refill, but if okay, add a little salt to the water.

✱ Reduce the heat further until the water is just simmering and cook for 15 minutes. Skim off any scum, then add all the vegetables, peppercorns, bay leaves, and garlic. Cook for another 2 hours 15 minutes.

✱ Turn the heat off and leave the hocks to cool, then chill in the fridge in their stock.

✱ The next day, preheat the oven to 400°F.

✱ Lift the chilled hocks out of the jellied stock and rinse off any jelly clinging to the hocks.

✱ Leaving the large bone in the meat, pull out the second smaller bone, then trim off the rind and discard. Lightly score the meat that's left and place on a non-stick baking sheet.

✱ Mix all the glaze ingredients together really well, then pour over the hocks and place in the hot oven. Cook for 20–25 minutes, spooning the glaze over repeatedly until well glazed.

✱ Serve in deep bowls and just pull off the meat in large chunks. I eat this hot or cold with buttery mashed potatoes.

Baked ham with spicy squash chutney ⇒

Baked ham with spicy squash chutney

THIS IS AN UNUSUAL WAY OF COOKING HAM. IT DOES TAKE A BIT OF TIME BUT IS WELL WORTH THE EFFORT—GREAT EATEN HOT OR COLD FOR BREAKFAST OR BRUNCH.

Serves 4-6   Preparation time 30 minutes   Cooking time about 2 hours 45 minutes–3 hours 15 minutes

about 6 cups all-purpose flour
³/₄ cup salt
about 10 large egg whites
3¹/₄lb smoked ham, rind on, soaked overnight and
   dried well
¹/₄ cup honey
1 tablespoon molasses
1 teaspoon ground allspice

CHUTNEY
¹/₄ cup good-quality olive oil
1 teaspoon caraway seeds
1 teaspoon crushed juniper berries
1 teaspoon whole cloves
2 small red onions, finely chopped
2 garlic cloves, crushed
1 tablespoon finely chopped fresh ginger
1lb peeled and seeded squash
¹/₂ cup cider vinegar
2 tablespoons Worcestershire sauce
³/₄ cup light brown sugar
salt and freshly ground black pepper

✱ Preheat the oven to 375°F.

✱ Sift the flour and salt into a bowl and stir in enough egg white to form a stiff dough. I keep leftover egg whites in the freezer, and this is a good way of using them up.

✱ Sit the ham on a thick wedge of scrunched-up foil in a roasting pan. Roll out the dough carefully on a lightly floured surface to a rectangle large enough to cover the top and sides of the ham. Lay the dough over the top, then tuck under the ham and press the edges together to seal well, ensuring the whole ham is encased. Make a small incision in the top to let out the steam.

✱ Bake for about 2 hours 30 minutes-3 hours. To check if it is cooked, insert a skewer through the vent—there should be little resistance but the meat shouldn't be too firm.

✱ Meanwhile, for the chutney, heat the olive oil in a large pan. Add the caraway seeds, juniper berries, cloves, onions, garlic, and ginger and cook for about 6-8 minutes—you'll get a wonderful smell all around the kitchen.

✱ Add the squash, vinegar, Worcestershire sauce, and brown sugar, stir in, and season well. Then cook slowly for about 15-20 minutes until the squash is tender and the consistency of the chutney is nice and thick. Let cool.

✱ Mix the honey, molasses, and allspice together and set aside.

✱ When the ham is cooked, remove the crust and discard. Years ago, some of the crust would have been grated and placed on top of the cooked ham (the forerunner to bread crumbs). Cut away all the rind and a little fat from the ham.

✱ Place the ham in a clean non-stick roasting pan, cut the fat into a crisscross pattern, and pour over the honey and molasses mixture.

✱ Increase the oven temperature to 425°F and slide the ham back into the oven to glaze nicely. Bake for about 15-20 minutes—watch closely, otherwise it will stick and burn.

✱ Cut the ham into thick slices and serve with the chutney or the compote on page 93.

Grilled ham steak with spicy chickpea & tomato stew

I REALLY LIKE HAM STEAKS. YES, I LIKE THEM WITH PINEAPPLE AND I ALSO LIKE THEM WITH FRIED EGGS AND HASH BROWNS. MY DAUGHTER ADORES THEM, BUT THE HAM HAS TO BE OF GOOD QUALITY, OTHERWISE IT IS TOO SALTY AND HAS NO FLAVOR. I ESPECIALLY LIKE THE RIM OF FAT; IT'S DELICIOUS AND WHEN DRY-CURED THE RIND WILL BUBBLE UP BEAUTIFULLY. HERE I HAVE ADDED A CHICKPEA AND TOMATO STEW, BOTH EASY AND FILLING.

Serves 4   Preparation time 10 minutes   Cooking time 15 minutes

¼ cup olive oil
2 onions, finely chopped
2 garlic cloves, chopped
1 x 14oz can chopped tomatoes in juice
1 x 14oz can chickpeas, drained
pinch of red pepper flakes
½ chicken or vegetable bouillon cube
¾ cup cold water
2 tablespoons vinegar (any type)
1 tablespoon sugar
4 ham steaks, about 10oz each
salt and freshly ground black pepper

✱ Heat the oil in a saucepan, add the onions and garlic, and soften for a couple of minutes.

✱ Add all the remaining ingredients except the ham and simmer for 10–15 minutes or so until the mixture thickens. Season well and add a little more olive oil if needed; the sauce should be glossy.

✱ Meanwhile, grill the steaks for 4–5 minutes on each side until cooked through, but don't overcook.

✱ To serve, pile the chickpea stew into the middle of four bowls and top each with a ham steak.

✱ This stew is also great cold with crusty bread as a dip or as a topping.

Baked ham with tomato compote

THE VICTORIANS LIKED SAVORY COMPOTES, ESPECIALLY AT BREAKFAST TIME, AND HERE IS A TOMATO ONE THAT I HAVE COOKED FOR YEARS TO SERVE AS AN ALTERNATIVE ACCOMPANIMENT TO THE BAKED HAM ON PAGE 90.

Serves 4-6   Preparation time 30 minutes   Cooking time about 2 hours 45 minutes–3 hours 15 minutes

1 quantity Baked ham (see page 90)

COMPOTE
½ cup cold water
½ cup cider vinegar
⅓ cup unrefined granulated sugar
1 teaspoon caraway seeds
1 cinnamon stick
2 shallots, finely chopped
1lb 2oz cherry tomatoes
2 tablespoons chopped tarragon

✽ While the ham is baking, prepare the compote. Put the water, vinegar, sugar, caraway seeds, cinnamon stick, and shallots into a saucepan and bring to a boil, then reduce the heat and simmer for 2 minutes. Add the tomatoes and cook for 1 minute, or until the skins just start to split. Turn off the heat and cover with plastic wrap. Let cool. When cool, add the chopped tarragon.

✽ Cut the baked and glazed ham into thick slices and serve with the compote, and perhaps a fried egg or two.

Ham hock salad with English mustard & lentil dressing

THIS DRESSING MUST BE MADE THE DAY BEFORE YOU NEED IT; IF YOU MAKE IT AND EAT IT IMMEDIATELY, IT'S AWFUL, BUT IF YOU LEAVE THE DRESSING FOR 24 HOURS, THE FLAVOR CHANGES DRAMATICALLY, BELIEVE ME. MUSTARD POWDER LOSES ITS PUNGENCY SOON AFTER YOU ADD LIQUID, SO IT'S BEST TO LEAVE THIS IN OVERNIGHT, BUT RE-SEASON WITH SALT AND PEPPER, SUGAR, AND VINEGAR THE NEXT DAY. WARM THE SMALL CHUNKS OF SUCCULENT HAM HOCK IN THE DRESSING.

Serves 4   Preparation time 20 minutes, plus cooling/chilling   Cooking time 2 hours 40 minutes

2 brined ham hocks (see page 85)
salt and freshly ground black pepper
1 teaspoon black peppercorns
3 bay leaves

DRESSING
2 egg yolks
2 heaping tablespoons English mustard powder
sugar, to taste
3 tablespoons white wine vinegar
1¼ cups vegetable oil
2 tablespoons cold water
4 shallots, finely sliced (not chopped)

4 heaping tablespoons fresh mixed herbs, such as basil, flat-leaf parsley, chives, chervil, and tarragon
¾ cup cooked green lentils

TO SERVE
1 small bag watercress
1 small head Romaine or Iceberg lettuce, chopped
4 tomatoes, cut into chunks
boiled new potatoes (if serving as a main course)

✱ Soak the ham hocks in cold water for 24 hours, changing the water occasionally.

✱ Drain the hocks and put into a large saucepan with plenty of fresh cold water. Bring to a boil and then you must reduce to a simmer, not keep at a raging boil, or the meat will become tough and stringy, especially the outside 1¼–1½in. A good tip here is to taste the water after simmering for 5 minutes. If it's salty, pour out the water and start again; if not, add a little salt and the peppercorns and bay leaves. Then simmer the hocks for 2 hours 30 minutes exactly.

✱ Remove the pan from the stove and let the hocks cool in the liquid, then chill in the fridge in the stock until cold.

✱ To prepare the hocks, remove them from the jelly and wash off under warm water. Remove all the skin and gristle and pull the lobes of meat off the bone. Remove most of the fat and cut the meat into bite-sized pieces.

✱ For the dressing, put the egg yolks, mustard powder, salt and pepper, sugar, and vinegar in a bowl. Whisk together, then gradually add the vegetable oil until completely emulsified. Check the seasoning and adjust if necessary. Also add the cold water to form a thick, but not too thick, mayonnaise. Stir in the shallots, herbs, and lentils.

✱ Cover and place the dressing in the fridge, leaving it overnight if possible. Then check the seasoning and adjust, with sugar, vinegar, salt, and pepper, stirring well.

✱ To serve, pour some of the dressing into a small pan, add a few pieces of ham hock, and warm through gently. Spoon this over a mixture of watercress and lettuce, mix well but carefully, pile onto a plate, and serve warm with the tomatoes. For a main course, serve with boiled new potatoes.

Easy potato & ham hash with arugula & apple salad

I LOVE HASH IN ANY FORM—NORMALLY BEEF IS USED, AND CORNED BEEF AT THAT. HERE IS A HAM VERSION THAT IS BOTH DELICIOUS AND REALLY EASY TO MAKE. I USE LEFTOVER ROAST POTATOES, BUT ANY COOKED POTATO WILL DO.

Serves 4   Preparation time 20 minutes   Cooking time about 30 minutes

¼ cup olive oil
1 onion, cut into ³⁄₄in chunks
2 large carrots, peeled, cooked, and cut into small pieces
8 leftover or cooked roast potatoes, cut into small chunks
½ cauliflower head, broken into florets, then cooked
1 chicken bouillon cube, crumbled
½ cup water
7oz cooked ham, cut into ½in cubes
freshly ground black pepper
4 fried eggs, to serve

SALAD
5½oz arugula (2 bags)
2 small apples, such as Cortland
1 small red onion, finely sliced
2 tablespoons olive oil
squeeze of lemon juice

✱ Heat the olive oil in a large, non-stick frying pan with a tight-fitting lid. Add the onion and cook for a few minutes to brown slightly.

✱ Add the carrots, potatoes, and cauliflower to the pan and continue to cook until they all take on a little color.

✱ Next, add the crumbled bouillon cube, water, cubed ham, and a generous dash of pepper, then bring to a boil. Stir well, cover with the lid, and cook over low heat for 20 minutes.

✱ When the vegetables are cooked, check the seasoning and adjust if necessary, then keep warm.

✱ For the salad, place the arugula in a large bowl, then grate the apples on a coarse grater, with the skin on. Add to the arugula and onion and mix well but lightly.

✱ Add the olive oil and lemon juice and mix well again, but be careful not to crush the arugula.

✱ Serve the hash in deep bowls, each topped with a fried egg, with the salad separately.

Pork osso bucco

I COOKED THIS RECIPE MANY YEARS AGO IN MY RESTAURANT. I WAS LOOKING FOR SOMETHING THAT USED A CHEAPER CUT OF MEAT AND THIS DISH CAME TO MIND. THE GOOD THING IS THAT IT CAN BE SIMMERED ON TOP OF THE STOVE VERY GENTLY, SO THE OVEN CAN STAY OFF, SAVING POWER. DO SIMMER IT VERY GENTLY; IT WILL MAKE ALL THE DIFFERENCE. I USE SOME OF THE BRAISING LIQUID IN THE FINAL SAUCE, SO BEWARE OF SEASONING TOO HEAVILY AT THE START.

Serves 4   Preparation time 30 minutes, cooling/chilling
Cooking time 2 hours 40 minutes for the osso buccos, 1 hour–1 hour 10 minutes to finish

8 cuts pork osso bucco (2in-thick slices of uncured
   pork shank—about 1 shank per serving)
about 2$\frac{1}{2}$ cups strong chicken stock (you may need less)
1 onion, finely chopped
1 carrot, peeled and finely chopped
1 celery rib, finely chopped
1 small sprig of fresh thyme
2 sprigs of fresh sage
2 garlic cloves, crushed
a few black peppercorns
pinch of salt

SAUCE
$\frac{1}{4}$ cup olive oil
2 onions, finely chopped
4 garlic cloves, chopped or crushed
1 x 14oz can chopped tomatoes in juice
1 x 6oz jar roasted peppers, drained and cut into
   $\frac{3}{4}$in cubes or slices
2 tablespoons tomato paste
2 chicken bouillon cubes
1 cup pork stock from cooking the osso bucco
$\frac{2}{3}$ cup dry white wine
$\frac{1}{4}$ cup sherry vinegar
2 tablespoons sugar
$\frac{1}{2}$ cup heavy cream
1 cup watercress, roughly chopped
salt and freshly ground black pepper

✱ Remove the rind and a little of the fat from the pork shank.

✱ Put the shank slices in a deep saucepan so that they fit nice and snugly. Cover with the stock until they are submerged by say 1in, and then add the vegetables, garlic, peppercorns, and salt.

✱ Bring to a boil and skim well, then cover, reduce the heat and just simmer, very slowly, for 2 hours 30 minutes, or until the meat is tender, succulent, but not falling off the bone.

✱ Once cooked, cool and chill well in the stock. When ready to finish the dish, remove the shank slices from the stock and measure out 1 cup of the stock for the sauce.

✱ To make the sauce, heat the olive oil in a saucepan, add the onions and garlic, and cook for 5 minutes to soften.

✱ Add all the remaining ingredients except the cream and watercress. Season, then simmer gently for about 35–40 minutes until reduced and a nice sauce consistency.

✱ Add the cream and cook for another 5 minutes. Finally, add the watercress and mix well, then re-season and taste to check the seasoning.

✱ Put the cooked osso buccos in a shallow saucepan and cover with the sauce, then simmer with the lid on for 15–20 minutes to warm through. Alternatively, put into an ovenproof dish, cover, and pop in the oven preheated to 350°F to heat through.

✱ Serve with steamed green vegetables such as beans, cabbage, or the best of what's in season.

CHAPTER 4 # Bacon & pancetta

I think it is safe to say that bacon is probably one of the most widely eaten pork products around the world. I remember fondly the first piece of bacon I ever cured, applying the cure ingredients and rushing in the next morning to see if it had turned that wonderful pink color we are so familiar with. It had, and I then set off on a journey that at times has had me pulling my hair out when it hasn't worked and at other times winning awards at national food competitions.

The all-American thick-cut bacon is cut from the belly—the fattiest part of the pig—which makes it delicious. Canadian bacon is cut from the loin and tends to be leaner than belly bacon, and back bacon—widely eaten in the UK and Ireland—is also from the loin. – Simon

BACON IS CURED USING ONE OF THE FOLLOWING PROCESSES:

Dry curing

The meat is rubbed with a mixture of curing salt, sugar, and sometimes spices. This mixture diffuses through the meat over a period of time, thereby curing the meat. This method is the slowest, but it produces the best-quality bacon.

Brine curing

Instead of the curing ingredients being applied directly to the meat, they are mixed with water to make a brine. The meat is then added and left to cure through. Again, this is a reasonably slow method that produces a quality product.

Brine injection

This method employs the use of a needle injector to force the brine into the meat. It's by far the fastest way to produce bacon and is the method most commonly used by large bacon producers because it results in a finished product in a short space of time—as little as 48 hours. In my opinion, the word "quality" should not be used to describe the end product but it is an economical way of curing bacon.

DRY CURING

This is my chosen method of curing bacon. Use loins or bellies ideally weighing 175–200lb. I prefer to use pigs of this size because they will give a fuller loin and belly so that after curing you are left with bacon slices that are of a decent size. If using a pH meter when selecting your meat, which I highly recommend, it needs to register between 5.5 and 5.8. This pH is usually reached three days after slaughter and is also an indication that microbiological growth is controlled. – Simon

Canadian bacon

YOU WILL NEED PER 2¼LB PORK LOIN:

2 tablespoons + 1 teaspoon curing salt (containing 1% sodium nitrite and 0.8% potassium nitrate)
¾ teaspoon dextrose (the heaviest of the sugars, which helps counteract the toughening effect of the salt)
½ teaspoon sodium ascorbate (the sodium salt of ascorbic acid, which helps to stabilize the cure color)
¼ teaspoon spice—black peppercorns, coriander seeds, juniper berries and bay leaves all work well in dry-cure mixes

✱ Mix these ingredients together thoroughly and apply to the pork, making sure the thickest part of meat receives the most amount of salt. Ensure that the whole piece of meat is covered with the mixture.

✱ Place in a suitably sized, robust plastic food container and leave to cure for 10 days in a cold fridge at a temperature of 34–38°F. During this time a brine will form in the bottom of the container, which should be discarded at regular intervals.

✱ After the 10 days, wash the bacon off in lukewarm water and let dry for a couple of hours in a cool, airy place.

✱ At this point you can smoke the bacon if you wish. If you do, the bacon needs to reach ambient temperature beforehand or you will get condensation and it will not smoke properly.

✱ Depending on the kind of smoker you have, the cooler the smoke, the better your bacon will be; I would recommend a smoking temperature of no higher than 108°F. Alternatively, simply leave it as it is.

✱ To keep your bacon in pristine condition, either vacuum pack it—a friendly butcher would do this for you I'm sure—or wrap the whole piece in parchment paper and keep in the fridge. Your bacon will improve with age, as the dehydration process intensifies its flavor, especially if you have used spices in your cure mix. You can then slice it as thickly or thinly as you prefer.

✱ Finally, and most importantly, when you get to make your first meal with your homemade Canadian bacon, please refrain from putting ketchup on it!

Thick-cut bacon

THE ONLY CHANGE TO THE INGREDIENTS ABOVE FOR CURING BELLY TO MAKE THICK-CUT BACON IS THE AMOUNT OF SALT REQUIRED—USE 2 TABLESPOONS + 1 TEASPOON CURING SALT PER 2¼LB BONELESS PORK BELLY. THE CURING TIME CAN BE SHORTENED TO 7 DAYS, BUT OTHERWISE FOLLOW THE METHOD FOR CANADIAN BACON ABOVE.

HOME SMOKING

The smell of fresh smoked bacon is every bit as appealing as the smell of freshly made bread. Although the practice of smoking food has been going on for more than 80,000 years, it's not as easy as one might think, and indeed is something of an art form. I use a commercially made smokehouse with hardwood chips such as beech and oak to smoke all of my products. It has a microprocessor to control every step of the smoking process, which ensures that my products are consistent every time. Home smoking, however, is a different breed altogether, being more of a case of trial and error. There are many smokers available to buy for home use, and many people devise their own smoking kit using old refrigerators and garbage cans. But as long as you are willing to persevere and record your methods, there is no reason why you shouldn't be successful.

To smoke your own bacon, you need to make sure that the bacon is sufficiently dry to take the smoke—it's advisable to allow your product to reach the same temperature as your smoker to avoid condensation. Depending on the smoker you are using, you can choose how long to smoke your bacon to achieve the desired color and flavor. – Simon

Smoked pancetta

THIS ITALIAN DELICACY, WHEN MADE PROPERLY, IS VERY DIFFERENT FROM WHAT IS GENERALLY OFFERED FOR SALE IN SUPERMARKETS. SMOKED BACON IS OFTEN SOLD AS PANCETTA AND, ALTHOUGH IT'S DELICIOUS, IT ISN'T PANCETTA. PANCETTA IS A CURED PORK BELLY MARINATED WITH HERBS AND SPICES, ROLLED AND TIED AND THEN STUFFED INTO A PERMEABLE CASING AND HUNG UP TO MATURE AND DRY MUCH LIKE A COPPA OR LOMO (SEE PAGE 81).

Makes 2¼lb

2 tablespoons + 1 teaspoon curing salt (containing 1% sodium nitrite
   and 0.8% potassium nitrate)
³/₄ teaspoon dextrose
¹/₂ teaspoon sodium ascorbate
2¹/₂ tablespoons dried thyme
2 teaspoons ground black pepper
2 teaspoons garlic powder
2¹/₄lb boneless, rindless pork belly or pig cheek (jowl)

✱ Mix all the dry ingredients together thoroughly and rub into both sides of the pork belly.

✱ Roll the belly into a cylindrical shape and tie to hold the shape. Let cure for a week in the fridge and then stuff into casing or wrap up in a pavé. Tie really tightly and prick with a needle to get rid of any air pockets.

✱ Apply a light smoke and hang up to dry in an environment with a temperature of 54–57°F and a relative humidity of 75–78 percent. It will be ready when quite firm to the touch, which will be in about 8–12 weeks' time.

Chile bacon

THIS BACON GIVES A LOVELY SPICY TWIST TO THE CLASSIC BLT (SEE PAGE 117). FOLLOW THE RECIPE FOR THICK-CUT BACON ON PAGE 105 BUT ADD ³/₄ TABLESPOON SMOKED PAPRIKA AND ³/₄ TEASPOON CHILE POWDER TO THE CURE BLEND.

Brickhill black bacon

THIS IS ONE OF THE SPECIALITIES OF THE HOUSE—SIMPLY DELICIOUS.

YOU WILL NEED PER 2¼LB DRY-CURED BACON:
1¾ cups water
½ cup molasses sugar
2¾ tablespoons curing salt (containing 0.6% sodium nitrite and 0.8% potassium nitrate)

✱ Mix the brine ingredients together thoroughly in a large, deep, strong plastic or stainless steel bowl or container—the easiest way is to use warm water and then chill the brine.

✱ Immerse your dry-cured bacon in the brine for 2–3 days, keeping it in the fridge—it should go nice and dark during this time.

✱ Remove the bacon and let dry for a couple of hours in a cool, airy place.

✱ Give the bacon a good smoke, after which it will resemble a large lump of coal. However, it will make the finest bacon sandwiches you have ever eaten.

American-style bacon

THE BEAUTY OF THIS TYPE OF BACON IS THAT WHEN YOU BROIL OR FRY IT, IT STAYS FLAT AND GETS REALLY CRISPY, JUST AS YOU WOULD FIND IN A NEW YORK DINER.

YOU WILL NEED PER 2¼LB BONELESS PORK BELLY:
2 cups water
3 tablespoons curing salt (containing 0.6% sodium nitrite and 0.8% potassium nitrate)
1 teaspoon dextrose
1 teaspoon sodium ascorbate

✱ Mix the brine ingredients together thoroughly in a large, deep, strong plastic or stainless steel bowl or container—the easiest way is to use warm water and then chill the brine.

✱ Immerse the belly in the brine for about 3–4 days, keeping it in the fridge.

✱ Remove the bacon and let dry for a couple of hours in a cool, airy place.

✱ Place the bacon in a smoker and hot smoke at 150°F until the core of the product reaches 130°F. Chill well and then slice thinly.

Smoked pig cheek pancetta with mussels & orzo

THE CHEEK OR JOWL IS A SOMETIMES FORGOTTEN PART OF THE ANIMAL, USUALLY ADDED TO SAUSAGES. HOWEVER, IT MAKES A GREAT PANCETTA WITH JUST THE RIGHT AMOUNT OF FAT. ADDING A LIGHT SMOKE ENHANCES THE FLAVOR EVEN FURTHER. THE ADDITION OF A RICH TOMATO SAUCE AND A FEW LIGHTLY STEAMED MUSSELS MAKES A PERFECTLY BALANCED, SLIGHTLY DIFFERENT DISH.

Serves 4   Preparation time 20 minutes   Cooking time 30 minutes

SAUCE
1/4 cup olive oil
1 large onion, finely chopped
2 garlic cloves, chopped
3/4 cup dry white wine
2 tablespoons tomato paste
1 x 14oz can chopped tomatoes in juice
2 ripe fresh tomatoes, chopped
2 tablespoons white or red wine vinegar
1 vegetable bouillon cube, crumbled
1 tablespoon sugar
salt and freshly ground black pepper

1/4 cup olive oil
3/4lb smoked cheek pancetta (see page 109),
   or use standard pancetta or smoked bacon, very thinly sliced
1 1/4 cups cooked orzo pasta
3/4lb cooked shelled mussels
1/4 cup chopped fresh basil
1/4 cup chopped fresh flat-leaf parsley

✱ For the sauce, heat the olive oil in a saucepan, add the onion and garlic, and cook for 3–4 minutes.

✱ Add the wine and tomato paste and cook for another 5 minutes, then add all the remaining sauce ingredients and season with salt and pepper. Cook down slowly for 10 minutes until thick and pulpy.

✱ Heat the olive oil in a wok or deep frying pan. Add the pancetta and stir-fry for 2–3 minutes, then stir in the tomato sauce and simmer for 5 minutes.

✱ Add the cooked orzo and mussels and just warm through. Finally, add the fresh herbs and season well. Serve immediately.

Simple spaghetti with pancetta, mozzarella, peas & olive oil

THIS BEAUTIFUL GREEN, TASTY SAUCE FOR SPAGHETTI IS SIMPLY MADE FROM FROZEN PEAS, VEGETABLE STOCK, FRESH MINT, AND EXTRA VIRGIN OLIVE OIL COMBINED WITH PANCETTA AND TOPPED WITH MOZZARELLA. THE END RESULT IS SURPRISINGLY GOOD, TRUST ME. PANCETTA, LIKE BACON, IS SALT-CURED PORK BELLY OR CHEEK, BUT IS SOMETIMES FLAVORED WITH HERBS AND ROLLED, AND AS WITH BACON IT CAN BE LIGHTLY SMOKED.

Serves 4   Preparation time 15 minutes   Cooking time 15 minutes

10$\frac{1}{2}$oz dried spaghetti (this will give you 6$\frac{1}{2}$ cups cooked)
7oz pancetta, very finely chopped
2 garlic cloves, crushed
1$\frac{3}{4}$ cups frozen peas
$\frac{1}{4}$ cup extra virgin olive oil
1 vegetable bouillon cube, dissolved in about $\frac{1}{2}$ cup boiling water
$\frac{1}{4}$ cup chopped fresh mint
salt and freshly ground black pepper
9oz pack fresh mozzarella, drained and diced

✱ Cook the spaghetti in a large saucepan of boiling water until just tender, then drain and keep hot.

✱ Heat a frying pan, add the pancetta, and cook until light and crispy. Add the garlic and cook, stirring, for 2 minutes.

✱ Meanwhile, cook the peas in plenty of salted boiling water for 2–3 minutes, then drain and keep warm.

✱ Pop half the peas into a blender, or crush with the back of a fork. Add the olive oil and pulse or mix, gradually adding enough of the stock to give you a nice sauce-like purée.

✱ Add the mint to the cooked spaghetti, along with the remaining whole peas and the cooked pancetta and garlic. Then add the hot pea sauce, stir well, and season with salt and pepper. Add the diced mozzarella and mix well.

✱ Serve with a simple tomato salad and garlic bread.

Bacon-aise sandwiches

I FIRST COOKED THIS DISH FOR A COMMEMORATION CEREMONY. IT WAS A COLD, WET, AND WINDY DAY AND THIS REALLY HIT THE SPOT. THE ADDED BONUS IS THAT IT USES INGREDIENTS YOU WOULD USUALLY HAVE ON HAND.

Serves 4   Preparation time 10 minutes   Cooking time 15 minutes

16 slices thick-cut bacon, 8 fried until really crisp,
   and 8 cooked normally, kept warm
6 tablespoons mayonnaise
1 scant tablespoon mango chutney or marmalade
1 tablespoon roughly chopped fresh flat-leaf parsley
1 heaping teaspoon prepared English mustard
8 slices seeded bread (any type will do)

✱ Finely chop the very crisp bacon and put into a bowl.

✱ Next, add the mayo, chutney or marmalade, parsley, and mustard and mix really well.

✱ Spread the bacon-aise liberally onto the bread slices. Top four of the bread slices with two warm bacon slices, then top with the remaining bread slices, bacon-aise-side down. Cut in half and serve.

Devils on horseback

I ONCE WORKED IN A HOTEL THAT SERVED SAVORY PLATES AFTER DESSERT. IT WAS A REAL PAIN BECAUSE YOU FINISHED WORKING A GOOD HOUR AFTER EVERYONE ELSE. HOWEVER, IT WAS NICE TO SERVE CLASSIC DISHES LIKE THE ONE BELOW, WHICH REPUTEDLY FIRST APPEARED IN PRINT IN 1888. THE PÂTÉ MAKES A BIG DIFFERENCE, GIVING THE END RESULT A MORE ROUNDED FLAVOR PROFILE.

Serves 4   Preparation time 10 minutes   Cooking time 10 minutes

8 ready-to-eat pitted prunes
3$\frac{1}{2}$oz pâté (any store-bought will do)
8 dry-cured smoked thick-cut bacon slices, cut as thinly as possible
2 tablespoons olive oil
1 lemon, halved, for squeezing over

✱ Open out the prunes slightly and spoon a little pâté into each, then close over as best as possible.

✱ Lay the bacon out on a cutting board and place a prune on the bottom of each slice. Roll up and secure with a half a wooden toothpick.

✱ Heat the olive oil in a non-stick frying pan, add the rolls, and cook for 2–3 minutes on each side. Serve warm with a squeeze of lemon.

BLT

THE COMBINATION OF CRISP BACON, SOFT BREAD, CRUNCHY LETTUCE, AND SWEET TOMATO IS A PERFECT MATCH OF TEXTURES AND FLAVORS, AND THE CONTRAST OF HOT BACON WITH COLD SALAD IS VERY SATISFYING. BUT HERE'S A TWIST ON THE GREAT CLASSIC. HEAT-CURED CRISP BACON (SEE PAGE 110) MAKES ALL THE DIFFERENCE AND, COUPLED WITH A CURRY MAYO, MOVES THE BLT TO CENTER STAGE. HEAT-CURED BACON CRISPS UP MORE EVENLY, MAKING THE SANDWICH MUCH NICER TO EAT, AND THE "CORONATION" MAYO IS A TIME-HONORED RECIPE THAT USES A SWEETENED CURRY POWDER SUPPOSEDLY INVENTED TO CELEBRATE QUEEN ELIZABETH II'S CORONATION.

Serves 2   Preparation time 15 minutes   Cooking time 15 minutes

8 slices thick-cut bacon
6 slices bread (your choice—try whole wheat, white, or sourdough)
3$^{1}/_{2}$ tablespoons soft butter
$^{1}/_{4}$ cup mayonnaise
1 tablespoon honey
$^{1}/_{2}$ teaspoon Madras curry paste
1 tablespoon chopped chives
2 large ripe plum tomatoes, thickly sliced
1$^{1}/_{2}$ cups Romaine lettuce, finely shredded
freshly ground black pepper

✽ Broil or fry the bacon until crisp but not burnt.

✽ Toast the bread on both sides, then butter well.

✽ Place two slices of toast on a cutting board and arrange four bacon slices on each.

✽ Mix the mayo, honey, and curry paste together well, then add the chives. Spoon half the mayo onto the bacon, then top with tomato slices.

✽ Add another slice of buttered toast to each sandwich, then the shredded lettuce and the remaining half of the mayo mixture. Season with a little pepper and top with the last pieces of toast.

✽ Cut into quarters on a diagonal, then secure each quarter with a toothpick. Serve warm.

Smoked bacon, sweet turnip & potatoes

I COOKED THIS DISH FOR THE FIRST TIME ON A BEACH IN NORTHERN NORWAY LAST YEAR. IT'S A VERY SIMPLE DISH BUT IT WORKS REALLY WELL, ESPECIALLY IF YOU ENSURE THAT THE BEST-QUALITY PORK IS USED. I ALSO ADDED SOME KING CRAB THAT I HAD CAUGHT AND SIMMERED IN OCEAN WATER RIGHT ON THE WATER'S EDGE, ITS SWEETNESS, AS WITH THAT OF THE TURNIP, GOING PERFECTLY WITH THE SMOKY BACON. SWEET TURNIPS ARE SOMETIMES EATEN RAW IN NORWAY, LIKE AN APPLE, BUT HERE I'VE COOKED THEM.

Serves 4   Preparation time 20 minutes   Cooking time 20–25 minutes

1lb 2oz slab smoked pork belly or bacon, chopped into 1in pieces
1 large onion, chopped
2 garlic cloves, crushed
1lb 2oz baby new potatoes, boiled and halved
9oz small sweet turnips, boiled, peeled and halved
salt and freshly ground black pepper
6 tablespoons mayonnaise
¼ cup chopped fresh dill

✳ Place a large dry sauté pan on the stove and heat until fairly hot.

✳ Add the pork belly or bacon to the hot pan. Cook for 5–6 minutes until the bacon has taken on a little color and the fat is starting to run. Remove from the pan and keep warm.

✳ Add the onion and garlic to the pan and again cook until a little color has been taken on, then add the potatoes and turnips and stir well.

✳ Return the meat to the pan and cook for 10 minutes, nice and gently. More fat will run, which is what you want, ensuring that all the ingredients take on a lovely color and are cooked through. Season well with pepper and a little salt.

✳ Remove the pan from the heat and spoon the contents into a large bowl, then dot with the mayonnaise and dill before serving.

Mussels with bacon & beer

I COOKED THIS DISH FOR THE FIRST TIME IN NAMIBIA ON AN OPEN FIRE CALLED A BRAAI—
A SORT OF OPEN BARBECUE. THE INGREDIENTS WERE SO SIMPLE BUT SUPERB, INCLUDING THE
LARGEST MUSSELS I HAVE EVER SEEN. COUPLED WITH THE LOCAL LIGHT BEER, TAFEL, IT MADE
A FANTASTIC LUNCH.

Serves 4   Preparation time 10 minutes   Cooking time 30 minutes

9oz smoked bacon, cut into $^1/_2$in cubes
1 large onion, finely chopped
2$^1/_4$lb fresh cleaned mussels (throw out any that refuse to close when firmly tapped)
salt and freshly ground black pepper
1$^1/_2$ cups lager

✱ Heat a large saucepan, add the cubed bacon, and cook
for 10 minutes, or until it is slightly browned and the fat is
starting to run.

✱ Add the onion and cook for another 10 minutes, again
until it has taken on a nice color.

✱ Add the mussels, a little salt and pepper, and the beer
and bring to a rapid boil. Stir well, cover, and cook for
6–8 minutes, stirring occasionally, until all the mussels are
open (throw out any that remain shut).

✱ Remove the pan from the stove, divide the mussels
between four deep bowls, and spoon the lovely smoky
beer liquid over the top. I serve this with crusty bread.

Mini bacon
& sweet corn fritters
with fresh tomato salsa

THIS IS GREAT, VERY EASY SNACK FOOD FOR BOTH KIDS AND ADULTS—MY KIDS LOVED THESE
FRITTERS WHEN THEY WERE GROWING UP. IT'S ALSO A GOOD WAY TO USE UP LEFTOVER BACON,
PORK, OR EVEN HAM—REALLY ANYTHING GOES HERE. THIS RECIPE MAKES 10–12 SMALL FRITTERS.

Serves 4   Preparation time 20 minutes, plus standing   Cooking time 15 minutes

2 whole eggs, plus 1 egg white
$^3/_4$ cup all-purpose flour, sifted
about $^1/_3$ cup milk
salt and freshly ground black pepper
4–6 slices thick-cut bacon
1 x 7oz can sweet corn kernels, drained
2 small shallots, finely chopped
pinch of ground cumin
1 tablespoon chopped fresh chives
vegetable oil, for frying

SALSA
7oz baby plum tomatoes, roughly chopped
$^1/_2$ red onion, finely chopped
2 tablespoons chopped fresh flat-leaf parsley
2 tablespoons olive oil

✱ Place the egg white in a large bowl and crack one of the
whole eggs into another bowl. Separate the remaining whole
egg and add the yolk to the bowl with the whole egg and
the white to the other bowl containing the white.

✱ Add the flour and a little over half of the milk to the whole
egg and extra yolk and mix together—this should keep
you from getting a lumpy batter (says he!). Gradually beat
in enough of the remaining milk to make a thick batter.
Season well with salt and pepper and let stand for about
20 minutes.

✱ Meanwhile, cook the bacon on both sides until crisp.
Let cool slightly, then cut into small pieces.

✱ For the salsa, mix all the salsa ingredients together in a
bowl and season with salt and pepper.

✱ Pour the sweet corn into a colander and use the back of
a spoon to gently squeeze out any excess water. Add to the
batter with the chopped shallots, bacon, cumin, and chives.

✱ Whisk the egg whites until stiff, then add to the batter and
fold together.

✱ Heat a little vegetable oil in a non-stick frying pan. Add
separate spoonfuls of the batter mixture and allow them
to spread slightly. Cook, in batches, over medium heat for
about 2–3 minutes, or until just set and golden brown on the
bottom, then turn over and cook the other side.

✱ Serve the fritters hot with the fresh tomato salsa.

Hot bacon, roasted garlic
& watercress salad

THIS SALAD MAY BE VERY SIMPLE, BUT IT'S ALSO VERY TASTY. THE SECRET IS TO HAVE EVERYTHING PREPARED BEFORE YOU BEGIN PUTTING IT TOGETHER—TRUST ME! DON'T BE ALARMED ABOUT THE AMOUNT OF GARLIC; ONCE COOKED IT WILL LOSE MOST OF ITS PUNGENCY. YOU CAN EITHER WHISK ALL THE DRESSING INGREDIENTS TOGETHER IN A BOWL OR PLACE THEM IN A CLEAN JAR, SCREW ON THE LID, AND SHAKE WELL TO COMBINE. DON'T ADD THE DRESSING TO THE SALAD UNTIL THE LAST MOMENT, OTHERWISE THEY WILL COLLAPSE AND WILT. TO EAT THE GARLIC CLOVES, JUST SQUEEZE THEM TO POP THE FLESH OUT OF THE SKINS.

Serves 4   Preparation time 20 minutes   Cooking time 20–25 minutes

2 heads of garlic
about 20 baby new potatoes, boiled and cooled
3 cups watercress
4^{1}/$_{2}$oz bag mixed green salad leaves
2 tablespoons vegetable oil
12 thick-cut bacon slices, cut into ^{3}/$_{4}$in pieces
salt and freshly ground black pepper

DRESSING
3 tablespoons good-quality extra virgin olive oil
2 teaspoons Dijon or whole-grain mustard
pinch of sugar
juice of ^{1}/$_{2}$ lemon

* Break up the heads of garlic so that all the cloves are separate, then cut off the hard root of each, but don't remove too much of the clove.

* Put the cloves in their skins into a small saucepan of salted boiling water and bring back to a boil. Reduce the heat and simmer for 3–4 minutes, or until they are very soft, then drain.

* Cut the potatoes in half lengthwise and put the watercress and salad leaves in a large bowl.

* Heat the vegetable oil in a wok or large frying pan, add the bacon, and cook slowly for 10–15 minutes, or until it starts to crisp up.

* Add the garlic (skins and all!) and potatoes and cook until they are all golden brown.

* Meanwhile, whisk the dressing ingredients together.

* Pour the dressing over the salad and toss well. Pile equal amounts of the garlic, potato, and bacon mixture onto plates, then pile the salad leaves on top. Serve immediately.

Baked potato, sweet cabbage & blue cheese layer cake

THIS IS A GREAT DISH, EASY TO PREPARE AND VERY TASTY. THE INGREDIENTS FORM THE BEDROCK OF IRISH FOOD, AND OVER THE CENTURIES THERE HAVE BEEN THOUSANDS OF RECIPES INVENTED USING THESE STAPLES. THE MELTING CHEESE COMBINES WITH THE COOKED POTATOES, BACON FAT, AND CABBAGE TO MAKE A ONE-POT MEAL THAT IS SO SATISFYING.

Serves 4–6   Preparation time 20 minutes   Cooking time about 1 hour 15 minutes

1 1/2 tablespoons unsalted butter
1 tablespoon olive oil
1/2 small Savoy cabbage, inner leaves only, very finely sliced
2 tablespoons vegetable oil, plus extra for oiling
7oz thick-cut bacon slices, chopped
1 1/4lb peeled medium potatoes, cut into 1/8in-thick slices
salt and freshly ground black pepper
1 cup blue cheese, roughly grated or chopped

✳ Preheat the oven to 400°F.

✳ Heat the butter and olive oil together in a large sauté pan, add the cabbage, and cook for about 15 minutes until softened. Drain well in a colander.

✳ Heat the vegetable oil in a frying pan, add the bacon, and cook until the fat runs. Drain in a colander with the cabbage and reserve the fat.

✳ Toss the potato slices in the reserved bacon fat. Place a layer of them, overlapping, in the bottom of a lightly oiled 11in non-stick ovenproof frying pan and season with a little salt and pepper. Spread over a little cabbage and bacon, then top with some of the cheese. This helps to keep the whole cake together. Continue overlapping and seasoning the potatoes and layering with the cabbage, bacon, and cheese.

✳ Place the pan on the stove and heat for a few seconds so that the potato starts to brown and bubble on the bottom.

✳ Cover lightly with foil and bake in the oven for about 50 minutes. Remove the foil and check whether the cake is cooked—you should be able to pierce it with a knife with no resistance. Replace the foil, then press down lightly to compact the cake.

✳ Let cool slightly, say 15 minutes, then turn onto a cutting board, cut into wedges, and serve with a small salad dressed with a little French dressing.

CHAPTER 5 Sausages

According to Mark Twain, "Those that respect the law and love sausages, should watch neither being made." This quote has stuck in my mind for 20 years, and I refer to it with alarming regularity when discussing the humble sausage. I believe sausage making is an art form, and I have no issue at all with anyone looking at how mine are made. In fact, I would actively encourage people to come and watch the process, as I think it's important that everyone is aware of what they are eating, especially when supermarkets are trying their hardest to make our food as cheap as possible.

For me, sausages are a massively personal subject and a really important part of my business. My recipes are extremely precious too, and have taken years to perfect, so rather than write prescriptive recipes, what follows are the fundamentals, so that you can adapt them to make them your own.

For too long, sausages were predominantly seen as an inexpensive way of feeding a family and a great way for butchers to use up meat scraps. This was never the philosophy adopted by countries like Spain and Germany, however. For them, the sausage has always been an important part of a butcher's repertoire, and the meat selection and quality control used in making them has left us trailing embarrassingly behind, in my opinion. However, with stricter food labeling and general food-quality awareness, we are at last catching up and even starting to produce some of the classics, such as bratwurst and Toulouse, to similar standards. As a rule, most European sausages contain only meat and water, or just meat, and therefore will have a much denser texture than some of the more familiar sausages. – Simon

Cooking sausages

COOKING SAUSAGES IS QUITE AN ART, AND IT REALLY DEPENDS ON A FEW FACTORS AS TO WHICH IS THE BEST WAY TO GO ABOUT IT. I WAS ONCE TOLD BY ANOTHER CHEF THAT YOU MUST NEVER PRICK A SAUSAGE; HE NEVER EXPLAINED WHY AND I'M NOT SURE WHY HE WOULD SAY THAT. I HAVE BEEN THINKING ABOUT IT FOR YEARS AND THE ONLY VIABLE REASON COULD BE THAT IT KEEPS THEM FROM EXPLODING.

* In my mind, there are four ways to cook a sausage: broiling, baking, pan-frying, and grilling. Some sausages, like the French *boudin blanc* (white chicken sausage) and *boudin noir* (blood sausage), are gently simmered. I prefer to cook sausages gently, then pop them into a hot oven or under a hot broiler, turning occasionally to get a good all-around color. This also ensures they do not split, unless you overcook them. And while we are on the subject, you must make sure you cook sausages perfectly, because they are horrible if under- or overcooked.

* It goes without saying that the base product has to be of good quality to start with. I have found that Simon's sausages cook perfectly; this could be due to the fact that they have a high percentage of meat, and of course fat, and even the right amount of filler to bind them. Too much filler and they are dry, too little and they fall apart. The skins make all the difference when cooking a sausage and Simon only uses natural skins; it has to help.

* One last point to highlight: NEVER deep-fry—this will make your sausages look and taste disgusting! — Phil

FRESH SAUSAGES

The British banger

THERE ARE THREE MAIN BUILDING BLOCKS TO A GOOD BRITISH-STYLE BANGER, OR SAUSAGE: TOP-QUALITY BELLY AND SHOULDER PORK (THE FAT CONTENT OF WHICH NEEDS TO BE 25 PERCENT); SEASONING (SALT AND GROUND WHITE PEPPER IS ALL YOU NEED TO START—FOR EVERY POUND OF MEAT YOU NEED 1 TABLESPOON SALT AND 1¼ TEASPOON WHITE PEPPER); AND BINDER (BREAD RUSK IS MY PREFERRED CHOICE, BUT MELBA TOAST WILL DO. 10 PERCENT OF THE TOTAL MIX IS PLENTY). THIS WILL MAKE A SUCCULENT PORK SAUSAGE WITH A WELL-ROUNDED FLAVOR, BUT WITH THE ADDITION OF SPICES YOU CAN TAILOR-MAKE YOUR OWN SPECIALITY SAUSAGES. THE FOLLOWING RECIPE GIVES THE MOST COMMONLY USED SPICES AND QUANTITIES.

1lb 10oz top-quality pork belly or shoulder (25% fat)
1 tablespoon cooking salt
½ tablespoon ground white pepper
3½oz bread rusk, melba toast, or 1 cup bread crumbs
⅔ cup chilled water
hog or sheep casings

PLUS ANY COMBINATION OF THE FOLLOWING, ACCORDING TO YOUR PREFERENCE:
¼ teaspoon dried sage
½ teaspoon ground nutmeg
½ teaspoon ground mace
¼ teaspoon ground ginger
2 teaspoons dried thyme
1 teaspoon paprika
large pinch of red pepper flakes, more or less to taste
1 teaspoon garlic powder
1 teaspoon ground black pepper (coarsely ground is best)

* In my mind, the single most important factor in the production of sausages is how they are put together. Make sure the pork is extremely well chilled and trimmed free of gristle and sinew. Then grind through a coarse plate, i.e. one with holes of ¼–½in in diameter, into a large bowl.

* In a separate bowl, add the seasoning to the bread rusk and mix well. Pour in the water and leave until the rusk has absorbed it all.

* Add the soaked rusk mixture to the meat and mix thoroughly until nice and tacky.

* Re-grind the meat through a ¼in plate, then stuff the sausage meat into either hog or sheep casings and twist into 4–5in links, or simply form into patties, then refrigerate for up to 2 days. You can also freeze them.

Pork with leek & stilton sausages

THIS IS A REALLY NICE, RUSTIC-LOOKING SAUSAGE, WHICH GIVES A WHOLE NEW MEANING TO A TOAD IN THE HOLE (SEE PAGE 141)!

Makes 2¼lb

1lb 10oz pork shoulder
1 tablespoon cooking salt
½ tablespoon ground white pepper
3½oz bread rusk, melba toast, or 1 cup bread crumbs
⅔ cup chilled water
about ⅓ leek, washed well, sautéed until soft, and cooled
⅓ cup Stilton cheese, crumbled
hog casings

✱ Grind the pork through a ⅓in plate into a large bowl.

✱ In a separate bowl, add the seasoning to the bread rusk and mix well. Pour in the water and leave until the rusk has absorbed it all.

✱ Add the soaked rusk mixture to the meat along with the leek and Stilton and mix thoroughly until nice and tacky.

✱ Stuff the sausage meat into hog casings and twist into 4–5in links.

Pork with apricot & ginger sausages

ANOTHER RUSTIC-STYLE SAUSAGE, WHICH IS GREAT ON THE GRILL.

Makes 2¼lb

1lb 10oz pork shoulder
1 tablespoon cooking salt
½ tablespoon ground white pepper
1 teaspoon ground ginger
3½oz bread rusk, melba toast, or 1 cup bread crumbs
⅔ cup chilled water
⅓ cup dried apricots, chopped
hog casings

Follow the method for the Pork with Leek & Stilton Sausages opposite, adding the ginger with the seasoning to the bread rusk and the chopped dried apricots to the meat with the soaked rusk mixture.

Cumberland sausage

THIS IS A VERY POPULAR BRITISH SAUSAGE AND THE MOST DISPUTED AS TO WHICH IS THE CORRECT RECIPE. THIS IS MY INTERPRETATION, BE IT RIGHT OR WRONG.

Makes 2¼lb

2lb pork shoulder
1 tablespoon cooking salt
½ tablespoon ground white pepper
1 teaspoon coarsely ground black pepper
¼ teaspoon rubbed sage
2oz bread rusk, melba toast, or ½ cup bread crumbs
¼ cup chilled water
hog casings

Follow the method for the Pork with Leek & Stilton Sausages opposite, adding the sage with the seasoning to the bread rusk. Then after stuffing into hog casings, instead of twisting into links, leave in lengths to make coils.

Italian sausage

IT IS THE FENNEL SEEDS THAT MAKE THESE ITALIAN. THEY ARE ONE OF MY PERSONAL SAUSAGE FAVORITES AND ARE DELICIOUS EITHER GRILLED OR SIMMERED IN A SPICY TOMATO SAUCE.

Makes 2¼lb

2¼lb pork shoulder
1 tablespoon cooking salt
1½ teaspoons cracked fennel seeds
¾ teaspoon ground white pepper
1 teaspoon hot paprika
¾ teaspoon garlic powder
large pinch of red pepper flakes
hog casings

✱ Grind the pork through a ⅓in plate into a large bowl—it is ground only once, but it's really important that there is no gristle at all.

✱ Combine all the dry ingredients and then mix with the ground meat thoroughly.

✱ Stuff the sausage meat into hog casings and twist into links, then refrigerate. They will keep in the fridge for a couple of days, but they also freeze well.

Bratwurst

BRATWURST IS A GENERIC NAME FOR ALL FRESH GERMAN SAUSAGES. THEY ARE TRADITIONALLY MADE WITH PORK AND VEAL, AND YOU WILL FIND EACH REGION IN GERMANY HAS ITS OWN STYLE, THÜRINGER AND NUREMBERG BEING TWO WELL-KNOWN EXAMPLES. THE MAJOR DIFFERENCE BETWEEN BRATWURST AND A BRITISH BANGER IS THAT BRATWURST DO NOT CONTAIN ANY BINDER, SUCH AS BREAD, WHICH GIVES BRATWURST A MUCH DENSER AND MEATIER TEXTURE. MY VERSION CONTAINS JUST PORK, AND THEY WORK REALLY WELL ON THE GRILL.

Makes 2¼lb

10½oz pork shoulder
1¼lb pork belly
1 tablespoon cooking salt
½ teaspoon sugar
¾ teaspoon ground white pepper
½ teaspoon ground nutmeg
½ teaspoon ground ginger
1½ teaspoons dried marjoram
¼ teaspoon ground mace
½ cup chilled water
hog casings
butter, for pan-frying (optional)

✳ Grind the pork through a ¼in plate into a large bowl.

✳ Combine the dry ingredients with the chilled water, then mix into the meat until it is fully absorbed and the mixture is nice and tacky.

✳ Re-grind through the ¼in plate and mix again to ensure that it binds together.

✳ Stuff into hog casings and twist into links of the desired size.

✳ Refrigerate the sausages for at least 12 hours to allow the spices to diffuse through the meat.

✳ Poach in simmering water for about 25 minutes, then drain and pat dry with paper towels.

✳ When you are ready to eat, cook in a little butter in a frying pan until brown, grill, or broil.

Nuremberg bratwurst

THIS IS THE ULTIMATE BRATWURST, DEMONSTRATING THE HIGH ART OF SAUSAGE MAKING. THERE IS NO ADDED WATER IN THIS SAUSAGE AND THE USE OF ONLY PORK COLLAR MAKES IT EXTREMELY HIGH QUALITY TOO. THEY ARE BEST EATEN BY THE DOZEN, WITH COPIOUS AMOUNTS OF GERMAN BEER!

Makes 2¼lb

2¼lb pork collar or shoulder
1 tablespoon cooking salt
³/₄ teaspoon ground white pepper
¼ teaspoon ground nutmeg
1³/₄ teaspoons dried marjoram
1 egg, beaten (to help with binding)
sheep casings

✱ Grind the pork through a ¼in plate into a large bowl (it is ground only once).

✱ Combine all the seasonings, add to the meat with the egg, and mix thoroughly until nice and tacky.

✱ Stuff the sausage meat into sheep casings, twist into links about 5in long, and refrigerate. I would always eat these the day after production. When you are ready to eat, cook in a little butter in a frying pan until brown.

Thüringer bratwurst

THURINGIAN SAUSAGES HAVE BEEN PRODUCED IN THE GERMAN STATE OF THURINGIA FOR HUNDREDS OF YEARS AND THERE ARE EVEN RECIPES DATING BACK TO 1613 STORED IN THE STATE ARCHIVES. MANY RECIPE VARIATIONS CAN BE FOUND THROUGHOUT THE REGION, BUT THEY ARE ALWAYS COOKED ON A GRILL AND SERVED ON AN OPEN ROLL WITH KETCHUP AND MUSTARD (AND THE ODD BEER OR TWO).

Makes 2¼lb

1½lb pork shoulder
10½oz pork belly
1 tablespoon cooking salt
³/₄ teaspoon ground white pepper
½ teaspoon ground caraway seeds
1³/₄ teaspoons dried marjoram
¼ teaspoon ground nutmeg
½ cup chilled water
hog casings

✱ Grind the pork through a ¼in plate into a large bowl (it is ground only once).

✱ Combine all the seasonings, add to the meat with the water and mix thoroughly until nice and tacky.

✱ Stuff the sausage meat into hog casings and twist into links about 6in long.

✱ The sausages can be grilled as they are or poached first and then grilled—poaching first and then chilling immediately will increase their shelf life.

Christmas sausage rolls

I LIKE SAUSAGE ROLLS WHEN THEY ARE NOT SOGGY, FATTY, AND UNDERCOOKED.
SO HERE IS A RECIPE YOU CAN DEPEND ON.

Makes 24   Preparation time 20 minutes, plus chilling   Cooking time 20–25 minutes

1lb 2oz puff pastry or filo dough
1 egg, beaten

FILLING
1lb 2oz good-quality sausage meat, not too fatty (15–20 percent is perfect)
1 cup dried apricots, finely chopped
3½oz cooked peeled chestnuts, finely chopped
2 tablespoons chopped fresh sage

✱ Combine all the filling ingredients in a large bowl and mix together well.

✱ Place the sheets of pastry on a board and cut into 2in-wide strips. Brush well with beaten egg.

✱ Using a piping bag, pipe the sausage meat onto the pastry strips, slightly to one side. Fold over and seal the edge well. Brush again with beaten egg, then chill well.

✱ When ready to cook, preheat the oven to 400°F.

✱ Cut the long rolls into 24 small rolls. Place on a baking sheet and bake for 20–25 minutes until browned, crisp, and cooked through.

Toad in the hole with onion gravy

A BRITISH CLASSIC, THE SECRET TO A DELICIOUS TOAD IN THE HOLE RECIPE IS TO USE AN OVENPROOF FRYING PAN AND TO KEEP THE BATTER ONLY ABOUT AN INCH DEEP IN THE MIDDLE OF THE PAN. THIS WILL ENSURE A WELL-RISEN, CRISPY SIDE AND A COOKED BUT SLIGHTLY SOFT BOTTOM. ALSO, THE OVEN MUST BE HOT. I LIKE TO SERVE THIS WITH ONION GRAVY AND/OR A LARGE DOLLOP OF MUSTARD.

Serves 2   Preparation time 15 minutes   Cooking time about 45 minutes

GRAVY (serves 4–6)
2 tablespoons olive oil
3 large onions, finely sliced
1¹/₂ cups red wine
1 teaspoon fresh thyme, chopped
1 tablespoon all-purpose flour
1¹/₄ quarts good strong beef stock
2 tablespoons redcurrant or grape jelly
salt and freshly ground black pepper

1 cup all-purpose flour
2 eggs, beaten
1¹/₄ cups milk
salt and ground white pepper
2 tablespoons olive oil
4 large sausages, spicy, Pork with Leek and Stilton (page 134), or Cumberland (page 135)

✱ Preheat the oven to 425°F.

✱ For the gravy, heat the olive oil in a saucepan, add the onions, and cook for 15 minutes to soften. Add the wine and thyme and cook down until almost evaporated. Stir in the flour and mix well, then blend in the stock and redcurrant jelly and cook gently for 20 minutes, or until thickened. Season well with salt and black pepper.

✱ While the gravy is cooking, make the toad in the hole. Sift the flour into a large bowl, make a well in the center, and add the eggs and half the milk to the well. Whisk slowly, gradually incorporating the flour from the edge of the bowl. Add the remaining milk and whisk well until smooth, then season with salt and white pepper. Let stand while you cook the sausages.

✱ Heat the olive oil in a 10in non-stick, ovenproof frying pan. Add the sausages and brown nicely all over. Pour the batter into the hot sausage pan and then quickly transfer to the hot oven. Immediately reduce the temperature to 400°F.

✱ Cook for 25–35 minutes, or until well risen and golden around the edge. Remove from the oven and eat immediately with the hot onion gravy.

Spicy sausages braised in red onion marmalade

THIS IS ANOTHER NICE AND VERY EASY WAY OF COOKING SAUSAGES, AND IT'S VERY SATISFYING. IT JUST HAS TO BE SERVED WITH MASHED POTATOES.

Serves 4   Preparation time 10 minutes   Cooking time 30 minutes

2 tablespoons vegetable oil
8 Cumberland sausage pieces, about 3¹/₂oz each (page 135)
6 red onions, very finely sliced
2 tablespoons dark brown sugar
2 tablespoons Worcestershire sauce
³/₄ cup red wine
2 tablespoons malt vinegar
salt and freshly ground black pepper

✻ Heat the vegetable oil in a large frying pan with a lid and brown the sausage pieces all over, then remove from the pan and set aside.

✻ Add the onions and brown well, then add all the remaining ingredients with a little salt and pepper.

✻ Cover and cook gently for about 20 minutes, or until the onions are soft. Remove the lid, return the sausages to the pan, and cook, uncovered, for another 10 minutes, or until the sauce is thick and syrupy, and coating the sausages really well. Serve with mashed potatoes.

CURED SAUSAGES

These are sausages made with meat that has been cured with salt and sodium nitrite. Cured sausages can be fermented and dried like salami and chorizo, emulsified like hot dogs and frankfurters, or simply coarsely ground and smoked like polish kielbasa.

My fascination with this subject began shortly after I bought my butchery business. At the time I didn't realize how popular cured sausages were around the world, or that they would grow hugely in popularity. Over the years I have tried hundreds of different recipes but these are mostly my first dalliances with cured sausages and remain my favorites. – Simon

Reddening is the fermentation process. When the sausages are first made, they will turn a horrible gray color. After 12–14 hours, however, the salt, sugars, and starter cultures will have started to work, and the sausages will become a lovely red color.

Tempering is when frozen meat is placed in a cold fridge running at 32–36°F and left to temper/defrost until it reaches a temperature of approximately 36°F.

Andouille

THIS IS MY VERSION OF THE CLASSIC LOUISIANA SMOKED SAUSAGE, WHICH IS USUALLY SEEN IN DISHES LIKE JAMBALAYA AND GUMBO. BUT I LOVE THEM SIMPLY COOKED ON THE GRILL WITH A NICE HONEY AND MUSTARD GLAZE.

Makes 2¼lb

2¼lb pork shoulder (completely trimmed of gristle and sinew)
1 tablespoon curing salt (containing 0.6% sodium nitrite)
2 teaspoons coarsely ground black pepper
³/₄ teaspoon chile powder
1 tablespoon finely chopped garlic (about 2 cloves)
½ cup chilled water
hog casings

✱ Grind the pork through a ¼in plate into a large bowl.

✱ Combine the dry ingredients and then mix into the ground meat with the garlic and water until thoroughly combined.

✱ Stuff the sausage meat into hog casings and twist into 4–5in links.

✱ Let the sausages dry at room temperature for an hour or so and then hot smoke at 170°F until a core temperature of 155°F is reached.

Brickhill
smoked sausages

THIS WAS THE FIRST SMOKED SAUSAGE I MADE, INSPIRED BY READING THE BIOGRAPHY OF A POLISH
SAUSAGE MAKER IN THE US. I HAVE ADDED ONE OR TWO MORE INGREDIENTS TO MAKE IT MY OWN.

Makes 2¼lb

2¼lb pork shoulder or butt, tempered (see page 144)
1 tablespoon curing salt (0.6% sodium nitrite)
1¼ tablespoons garlic powder
1 teaspoon ground white pepper
½ teaspoon hot chile powder
2½ tablespoons honey
hog casings

✱ Grind the pork through a ⅓in plate into a large bowl (it is ground only once).

✱ Mix the ground meat with the curing salt, seasonings, and honey thoroughly until it becomes really sticky and tacky.

✱ Stuff the sausage meat into hog casings, twist into links, and refrigerate overnight to allow the spices to diffuse through the meat.

✱ Hang the sausages in a smoker until they reach room temperature and the skins are dry, then apply smoke until the desired color is obtained (see opposite).

✱ Simmer or steam the sausages at 175°F until an internal temperature of 160°F is reached for at least 2 minutes.

✱ Hang the sausages in the fridge for 3 hours to cool. Alternatively, you can hang them in a cool, airy place to air dry for a week, which really intensifies the flavor and also prolongs the shelf life.

SALAMI

Raw, fermented salami has been produced around the world for hundreds of years and is considered to be an art form. It was the knowledge and expertise passed down through generations that traditionally ensured that quality products were produced. Today, however, with regulation and constant food-safety awareness, modern technology plays a big part in salami production, although we still need the expertise!

Salami manufacture consists of three stages:

1. Production & stuffing

Selecting the appropriate meat is paramount when producing salamis. I prefer to use shoulder muscles from a mature female pig that have been trimmed of all soft fat and gristle, so that you have virtually 100 percent lean meat, and the hard fatback that is found on the neck of the pig. The ratio is usually 85 percent lean meat to 15 percent fat. The meat and fat are frozen and then left to temper in the fridge until it reaches a temperature of 28°F (see page 144). I prefer to grind the meat through a $1/3$ in plate on the grinder and mix in the curing ingredients by hand, as this gives the final product a lovely rustic homemade look that is so desired these days (especially by Phil). The salami can then be stuffed into the casings. I use ox runners (part of the bovine large intestine) because they are not too wide and, being natural, will dry uniformly and relatively quickly to give that true artisan look, but if unavailable, you can use your preferred casing.

2. Fermentation

This is the process by which the predominantly raw sausage is turned into a microbiologically- and shelf-stable product. Starter cultures are added to the mix before being stuffed into casings, and the stuffed salami is then subjected to temperatures of 72–79°F and a relative humidity of 90–93 percent for a period of 12–16 hours. This encourages the cultures to grow and produce lactic acid, which together with the presence of sodium nitrite in the curing salt, helps to drop the water activity and pH value of the salami and in turn contribute to its microbiological stability. If the fermentation process has worked correctly, the salamis will have turned a lovely red color and will be slightly firm to the touch. However, if you are making salamis to sell, investing in a pH meter is the only way to verify that this process has occurred—they should exhibit a pH of around 5 if they have fermented properly.

3. Drying & maturation

This is the stage during which we want the salami to lose a certain amount of moisture in a relatively short period of time without drying too quickly around the outside and hardening the case. As a rule of thumb, this process is usually achieved at a temperature of 54–59°F and a relative humidity of 72–78 percent with a minimal amount of airflow (zero airflow will encourage the growth of mold). Ideally, you are looking for a weight loss of approximately 30 percent before the salamis will be ready.

"Twiggies"

THESE SNACK SALAMIS WERE THE PRODUCT OF MY FIRST VENTURE INTO SALAMI MAKING. ONCE I HAD FINISHED MAKING THEM I REMEMBER THINKING THAT THEY WOULD NEVER REDDEN UP, BUT THEY DID AND I WAS HOOKED! A STARTER CULTURE (SEE PAGE 199) IS CRUCIAL TO THE FERMENTATION OF SALAMI. IT CONSISTS OF SELECTED BACTERIA THAT FERMENT SUGARS AND PRODUCE LACTIC ACID, PROVIDING THE PRONOUNCED SALAMI FLAVOR AND ALSO AIDING COLOR DEVELOPMENT AND THE MICROBIOLOGICAL STABILITY OF THE FINAL PRODUCT.

Makes 2¼lb (10-12 sausages)

1lb 10oz pork shoulder, tempered (see page 144)
9oz pork belly, tempered (see page 144)
1½ tablespoons curing salt (containing 0.6% sodium nitrite)
½ tablespoon ground white pepper
¾ teaspoon glucose
½ teaspoon sodium ascorbate
¼ teaspoon starter culture (see Glossary, page 199)
sheep casings

✱ Grind the tempered pork through a ¼in plate into a large bowl (it is ground only once).

✱ Combine all the dry ingredients and mix thoroughly with the pork.

✱ Stuff the sausage meat into sheep casings and twist into links.

✱ Hang the sausages in a warm, humid environment at a temperature of about 77°F for about 12 hours—an airing cupboard with some damp towels is ideal. During this time the sausages will redden and begin to dry.

✱ Next, move the sausages to an environment with a temperature of 54-59°F and a humidity of about 78 percent with little airflow—a cellar or pantry would work well. They should be ready to eat in about 10 days.

Snack chorizos

THIS IS A WONDERFUL VERSION OF THE SPANISH CLASSIC. THE SAUSAGES ARE MADE IN EXACTLY THE SAME WAY AS THE TWIGGIES BUT WITH SWEET, SMOKED AND HOT PAPRIKA AND GARLIC POWDER ADDED TO THE SEASONINGS—SEE BELOW FOR THE COMPLETE LIST OF INGREDIENTS.

Makes 2¼lb

1lb 10oz pork shoulder, tempered (see page 144)
9oz pork belly, tempered (see page 144)
1½ tablespoons curing salt (containing 0.6% sodium nitrite)
1½ tablespoons smoked paprika
1 tablespoon hot paprika
½ tablespoon ground white pepper
1½ teaspoons sweet paprika
¾ teaspoon glucose
¾ teaspoon garlic powder
½ teaspoon sodium ascorbate
¼ teaspoon starter culture (see Glossary, page 199)
sheep casings

Follow the method for "Twiggies" above.

Hot dogs

THESE HOT DOGS ARE INSPIRED BY THE CLASSIC GERMAN FRANKFURTER. I HAVE TWEAKED THE SEASONING AND TEXTURE OF THE SAUSAGE MEAT A LITTLE TO CALL IT MY OWN. TO MAKE CHEESY DOGS, USE THE SAME INGREDIENTS AS BELOW BUT ADD ¾ CUP FINELY DICED CHEDDAR TO THE MIX WITH THE DRY INGREDIENTS, AND FOLLOW THE SAME METHOD.

Makes 2¼lb

1lb 2oz pork butt/shoulder
10½oz pork belly
1 tablespoon curing salt (0.6% sodium nitrite)
¾ teaspoon ground white pepper
1 teaspoon paprika
½ teaspoon garlic powder
½ teaspoon ground nutmeg
½ teaspoon ground mace
¼ teaspoon ground ginger
¼ teaspoon chile powder
¾ cup chilled water
hog casings

✱ Grind the pork through a ⅓in plate into a large bowl.

✱ Combine the dry ingredients and mix into the meat, slowly adding the water until the mixture is really sticky and tacky.

✱ Re-grind the mixture through a ¼in plate.

✱ Stuff the sausage meat into hog casings and twist into links, then smoke as for the Brickhill smoked sausages and simmer or steam (see page 146).

HOT DOG SERVINGS

Serving hot dogs really is a very personal thing. I tend to stick to the basic staples and never really stray away, so that means sautéed onions, long and slow with a little salt, pepper, and sugar. Next, yellow mustard—absolutely. Ketchup? Yes, but not too much. Finally, cheese. Yes, love it or hate it— partially melted is the way to go. And of course there's the chili dog—a bit difficult to eat but a delicious classic!

Sausage, chorizo & bean casserole

THIS IS SO SIMPLE TO MAKE BUT PACKED FULL OF VEGETABLES AND FLAVOR. ANY SAUSAGE WILL DO, BUT THE ADDITION OF THE CHORIZO GIVES THE DISH A REAL KICK OF COLOR AND FLAVOR.

Serves 4   Preparation time 20 minutes   Cooking time about 50 minutes

2 tablespoons oil (any type will do)
14oz prime pork sausages
7oz chorizo, skin removed and cut into ⅛in slices
2 tablespoons tomato paste
2 red onions, sliced
2 garlic cloves, chopped
2 red bell peppers, seeded and roughly chopped
2 celery ribs, roughly chopped
1 x 14oz can tomatoes
1 x 14oz can red kidney beans, well rinsed
2 tablespoons vinegar
2 tablespoons soft brown sugar
3 bay leaves
about 1¼ cups strong chicken stock
2 tablespoons cornstarch

✱ Preheat the oven to 400°F.

✱ Heat the oil in a large ovenproof pan with a lid, add the sausages, and brown well. Add the chorizo and tomato paste and mix well.

✱ Add all the remaining ingredients except the cornstarch and mix together thoroughly. Cover and cook in the oven for 35–40 minutes.

✱ Remove the dish from the oven and uncover. Bring to a gentle simmer on the stove. Blend the cornstarch with a little cold water, then stir into the dish and cook, stirring, until thickened. Serve with mashed potatoes.

CHAPTER 6 Offal

any years ago, offal, or the "odd bits," as I call them, were used all the time. Every part of the pig was consumed in some way, shape, or form, apart from the toe nails and the squeak! In my very first cookbook, given to me in the early 1970s, I have two recipes handwritten by me. The first is for one of my dad's favorite dishes of all time, bread pudding. The second is a recipe for brawn, or head cheese as the French like to call it. I vividly remember my dad boiling this huge pig's head, with onions and peppercorns, then cooling and removing all the bits of flesh, cartilage, brain, and tongue. Everything would be carefully chopped with onions and the stock reduced, then packed into a clear Pyrex bowl and chilled. My mother hated it, but my dad, my brothers, and I all loved it; in fact, I still love it to this day.

So when it comes to cooking extremities and other odd bits I am very at home, although they really aren't Simon's cup of tea. This is probably where butchers and chefs don't see eye to eye. We have had many a conversation as to why he hates offal, and we never agree. From my point of view, with some careful thought and a bit of prep, all these bits can be really tasty.

Let's start from the front, with snout. Okay, it's not often used, but with simple preparation and cooking it can be turned into something quite delicious. Layered with potato, onions, bacon, and stock, cooked really slowly, the soft cartilage melting into a truly great dish.

Even my 12-year-old daughter likes it.

With the outbreak of BSE, or mad cow disease, brain, admittedly never hugely popular, disappeared off the menu but it is now making a comeback. I love it gently poached, then coated in a light batter and fried—its creamy texture works perfectly with crunchy ingredients such as raw vegetables or Iceberg lettuce. Cheeks, on the other hand, are very trendy now. This small nut of meat braises beautifully with cider and onions, but can also be cured, pancetta style, and thinly sliced, eaten raw, or lightly sautéed. Ears have always been a favorite of mine; twice cooked, Chinese style, they have a great texture and gelatinous mouth feel. I once had them on my menu as a mid-course, and they were hugely popular, partly because I didn't charge for them—just a nice thing to do, I thought. After that, they became a staple. The same careful treatment of tongues, hearts, liver, and kidneys also pays huge dividends.

Which brings me, finally, to pork rind or crackling. Yes, out of all the recipes in the book, this is the one that took the longest to get right. It takes a few hours to prepare, and some (Simon included) might think it's a lot of effort to go to for a bit of old pork skin, but for the hardcore people who enjoy this most comforting of foods, it very definitely is worth it. I LOVE IT! Drizzled with a little malt vinegar and sprinkled with salt, or dipped into a bowl of sharp apple compôte, there is nothing better to eat with a glass of chilled hard cider. – Phil

Pressed tongue in parsley peppercorn jelly

TONGUE IS NOT EVERYONE'S CUP OF TEA I KNOW, BUT TO ME IT'S ONE OF THE BEST PARTS OF THE PIG. PIG'S TONGUES ARE A THIRD OF THE SIZE OF AN OX TONGUE, BUT WITH A FINER TEXTURE AND FLAVOR. WHEN I WAS COOKING PROFESSIONALLY, WE WOULD COOK 4–6 OX TONGUES PER WEEK AND THEY WERE ALWAYS A HIT AT LUNCHTIME. WE WOULD MAKE A SHARP GHERKIN SAUCE FINISHED WITH A DASH OF CREAM TO SERVE WITH IT, SLICED OVER MASHED POTATOES. A MORE REFINED VERSION CONSISTED OF THE TONGUE FINELY SLICED WITH A LIGHT MADEIRA SAUCE ALONG WITH PEELED GRAPES AND TOASTED ALMONDS. I EVEN ENCOUNTERED A LADY WHO WANTED THE GRAPE VERSION FOR HER DOG'S DINNER! HERE, PIG TONGUE IS SIMPLY COOKED AND SET IN A JELLY TO GRACE THE LUNCH TABLE.

Serves 6–8   Preparation time 15 minutes, plus 4–5 days' curing, then chilling   Cooking time about 2 hours 15 minutes

CURE

1 quart water

¹⁄₂ cup curing salt (containing 0.6% sodium nitrite)

4 large pig's tongues, washed well

1 trotter, cleaned and washed really well

2 carrots, peeled but left whole

2 onions, peeled but left whole

2 celery ribs

1 small leek, trimmed and washed but left whole

¹⁄₄ cup vinegar

a few black peppercorns, plus a few extra

a few fresh parsley stalks, plus a few extra leaves

4 bay leaves

salt and freshly ground black pepper

✱ To cure the tongues and trotter, put the water and curing salt into a large plastic or stainless steel bowl or container and mix well—the easiest way is to use warm water and then chill the cure. Add the tongues and trotter and mix really thoroughly. Make sure they are covered with the water—I use a saucer to keep them submerged.

✱ Leave in the refrigerator for 4–5 days, turning the tongues occasionally.

✱ Wash the cured tongues and trotter really well in plenty of fresh cold water.

✱ Put the cured tongues and trotter into a saucepan and add all the remaining ingredients except the extra peppercorns and parsley leaves. Bring to a boil, then reduce the heat and simmer gently for about 2 hours, or until a skewer can pass through the thickest part of the meat with little resistance.

✱ Once the tongues are cooked, use rubber gloves to remove them from the cooking liquid. Carefully peel the skin from the hot tongues with your fingers—you must do this while they are still hot, or the skin won't come off.

✱ Remove the trotter and keep for another recipe, such as the Twice-cooked Trotters with Mango Chutney Glaze on page 165 (my dad would love to chew on it just as it is). Discard the vegetables and then gently simmer the cooking liquid for about 10 minutes until it is reduced by half, tasting to check that it's not too salty. This will ensure that the jelly from the trotter will set perfectly.

✱ Put the tongues into a small bowl and pack in well. Season the reduced stock, add the extra peppercorns and a few parsley leaves, and then pour over the tongues. Chill until set.

✱ Serve sliced with crusty bread and a few pickles such as gherkins, capers, and a little roasted garlic mayonnaise. The jelly will be delicious and so will the tongue.

Tail soup with jumbo couscous & cabbage

JUMBO OR ISRAELI COUSCOUS IS SOMETHING I DISCOVERED MANY YEARS AGO. THE GRANULE IS LARGE, WITH AN ALMOST PEARL-LIKE SHAPE AND HAS A DELICIOUS TEXTURE WHEN COOKED. IT MAKES A NICE CHANGE FROM THE STANDARD VARIETY OF COUSCOUS AND WORKS REALLY WELL IN SOUPS AND STEWS.

Serves 4   Preparation time 30 minutes   Cooking time 2 hours 30 minutes

10 pig's tails
1 pork hock, fresh, smoked, or brined (see page 85)
2 large carrots, peeled and chopped into medium-sized pieces
2 celery ribs, chopped into medium-sized pieces
2 large onions, chopped into medium-sized pieces
1 leek, trimmed, washed well and chopped into medium-sized pieces
2 bay leaves
1 teaspoon black peppercorns
a pinch or two of salt
¾ cup jumbo or Israeli couscous
2 chicken bouillon cubes, crumbled
½ small white cabbage, finely sliced

✱ Remove any hairs from the tails by using a kitchen blowtorch or holding over a gas flame with tongs. Then wash the tails and the hock well.

✱ Put the tails and hock into a large saucepan, cover with cold water, and bring to a boil. Then reduce the heat and simmer gently for 5 minutes, skimming off any foam.

✱ If using brined hocks, taste the water and replace with fresh water if it is too salty. Then add all the vegetables, bay leaves, peppercorns, a little salt, couscous, and bouillon cubes, and return to a boil.

✱ Reduce the heat and cook gently for 2 hours 15 minutes, or until the hock is cooked and you can remove the second smaller bone (the larger bone should stay put). You may have to add more boiling water every so often. The water should be gently simmering; if the hock cooks too quickly, the outside meat will become really dry and stringy before the center is cooked.

✱ Once cooked, remove the tails and hocks and let cool slightly. Meanwhile, add the cabbage to the pan and bring to a boil, then simmer for 5 minutes.

✱ Remove the fat and skin from the hock, then roughly chop the meat and add to the soup. Do the same with the tails.

✱ Return to a boil and taste—the soup should be like a minestrone or ribollita in consistency, i.e. nice and thick with vegetables, meat, and couscous. Serve the soup in deep bowls with crusty bread.

Twice-cooked trotters with mango chutney glaze

TROTTERS ARE QUITE IN VOGUE NOW IN PARTS OF THE US AND UK, BUT THEY ARE ALSO USED EXTENSIVELY IN EAST ASIA, ITALY, AND EVEN SPAIN. MY FATHER ALWAYS LOVED THEM BOILED WITH VINEGAR AND SALT AND PEPPER. TO ME THERE IS SOMETHING QUITE COMFORTING IN THE LOVELY JELLY AND SOFT TEXTURE OF THE TENDONS AND MEAT. WHICHEVER RECIPE YOU USE, YOU WILL NEED TO COOK THEM RIGHT THROUGH FIRST. SIMMERING WORKS FINE, AND SO DOES BAKING THEM IN A LOW OVEN. I USE BOTH METHODS; IT'S REALLY UP TO YOU. THIS DOES TAKE A COUPLE OF HOURS, BUT IT'S WELL WORTH THE WAIT. THE MANGO GLAZE IS A PERFECT FOIL FOR THE RICH MEAT.

Serves 4   Preparation time 25 minutes, plus soaking, cooling/chilling   Cooking time about 3 hours in total

4 large trotters, washed well
2 cups good-quality chicken or pork stock, or 2 cups water and 2 chicken or pork bouillon cubes, crumbled
2 large onions, peeled and cut into wedges
a few sprigs of fresh thyme
salt and freshly ground black pepper
1 head of garlic, sliced in half horizontally

GLAZE
³/₄ cup mango chutney or any other sweet fruit chutney or relish
2 tablespoons tomato paste
2 tablespoons cider vinegar
1 small red chile, finely chopped
4 garlic cloves, finely chopped
¹/₄ cup olive oil

✱ Soak the trotters in cold water for a couple of hours. Then preheat the oven to 350°F.

✱ Place a deep, ovenproof pan with a tight-fitting lid on the stove and add the drained trotters. Add the stock or water and bouillon cubes, onions, thyme, salt and pepper, and garlic and bring to a boil. Leave for 2 minutes, then cover.

✱ Transfer to the oven and cook for 1 hour 30 minutes. At this point, remove from the oven and gently turn the trotters over; they will probably have started to split due to the tendons contracting. Re-cover and return to the oven for another hour, maybe slightly longer, until soft.

✱ Once cooked, let cool and then chill well.

✱ When ready to re-cook, remove the trotters from the jelly (keep the jelly to form a fabulous soup base, perhaps for the Tail Soup with Jumbo Couscous & Cabbage on page 162) and place in a small roasting pan large enough to accommodate all four trotters with about a 1-in gap between them.

✱ Preheat the oven to 400°F.

✱ Make up the glaze by whisking all the ingredients together, then spoon over the trotters. Cook in the hot oven for 15–20 minutes, by which time they will be glazing nicely, although you will probably find that the glaze may be slightly runny at the start, as some of the jelly will ooze out of the trotters. Turn the trotters over and reglaze with a spoon until all the glaze has stuck to the trotters.

✱ When deeply glazed, remove from the oven and let cool for 10 minutes, then dive in. No knives and forks, just fingers and bibs!

Warm liver parfait with crunchy rye topping

THIS IS A SIMPLE PARFAIT, OR VERY FINE MOUSSE, THAT WORKS WELL WITH ALL LIVERS. THE SECRET IS TO ACHIEVE AS SMOOTH A PURÉE AS POSSIBLE AT ROOM TEMPERATURE SO THAT WHEN YOU ADD THE WARM BUTTER IT WILL HOMOGENIZE PERFECTLY. IF THE LIVER IS TOO COLD, AS IN STRAIGHT FROM THE FRIDGE, THE WARM BUTTER WILL SET IMMEDIATELY, GIVING YOU A SPLIT EFFECT RATHER THAN A PERFECTLY SMOOTH END RESULT.

Serves 4   Preparation time 20 minutes, plus cooling   Cooking time about 1 hour

9oz, or about 8 slices fresh rye bread, cut into cubes
³/₄ cup port
³/₄ cup chicken stock
14oz pig's liver, without tubes and skin, at room temperature, chopped
1 egg
12oz (3 sticks) unsalted butter, melted and warm but not hot
salt and ground white pepper

✱ Preheat the oven to 375°F.

✱ Place the rye bread in a food processor and process into fine crumbs—you are not looking for dust, just a rough, even crumb similar to a crumble topping.

✱ Spread out the bread crumbs on a baking sheet and place in the oven to dry thoroughly until crunchy—this should take 20–25 minutes, stirring occasionally. Let cool.

✱ Meanwhile, pour the port and stock into a saucepan and bring to a boil, then cook over medium heat until reduced by three-quarters. Let cool.

✱ Put the liver into a blender along with the cooled port and stock mixture and pulse-blend until really smooth. Add the egg and pour in the melted butter on medium speed (too much speed and for too long will make the parfait too light and moussey, and it will rise like a soufflé and also collapse like one).

✱ Strain the mousse through a sieve and season well with salt and white pepper.

✱ Mix well and then pour into four individual ramekins. Cover each one with a small piece of foil, then place in a deep roasting pan. Fill the pan half full with boiling water and carefully transfer to the oven. Cook for 35–40 minutes, or until the parfait is just wobbly and set; do not overcook.

✱ Remove from the oven and remove the ramekins from the water with a cloth. Let set for 5 minutes, then sprinkle with a nice topping of the rye bread crumbs and serve immediately.

✱ This parfait also works well cold pâté-style with Melba toast.

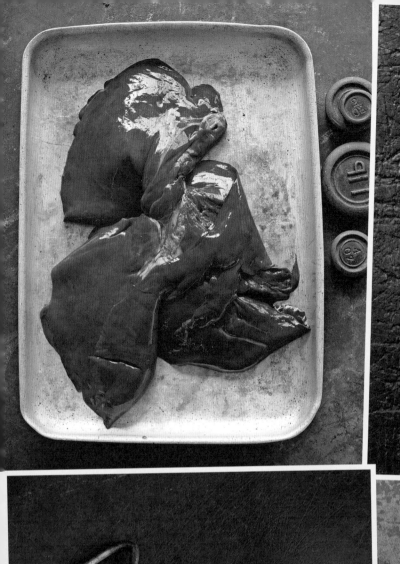
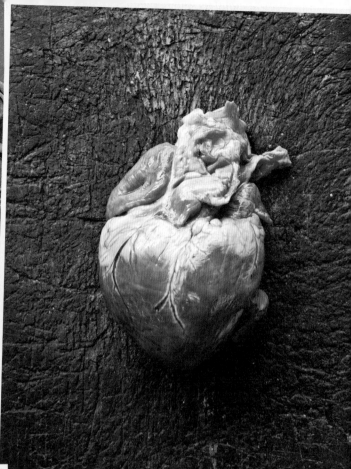

Pâté

A PRODUCT THAT IS MADE WORLDWIDE, PÂTÉ IS A BIT LIKE BLACK LICORICE—YOU EITHER LOVE IT OR HATE IT. THE PREDOMINANT INGREDIENT IS USUALLY LIVER AND MY VIEW IS THAT MOST OF THE COMMERCIALLY AVAILABLE PÂTÉS CONTAIN FAR TOO MUCH OF IT (PROBABLY BECAUSE IT COSTS NEXT TO NOTHING). MY FAVORITE SORT IS AN INTERPRETATION OF A GERMAN COUNTRY PÂTÉ CALLED *BAUERNLEBERWURST* (FARMER'S LIVER SAUSAGE).

Makes 2¼lb

1½lb fatty pork belly, cooked and still hot—I usually cook the meat
   in an oven bag to retain all the cooking juices for the pâté
10½oz pig's liver, without tubes and skin
1¼ tablespoons curing salt (containing 0.6% sodium nitrite)
3g fee (emulsifying agent—see Glossary, page 198)
¼ cup gutsleberwurst (liver sausage seasoning, available from good butchers)
2 eggs, beaten
sausage casings, optional

✱ Grind the cooked belly and liver through a ¼in plate
into a large bowl. Add the cooking juices and all the other
ingredients, except the casings, and mix very thoroughly.

✱ Dispense into foil pans or terrines and wrap tightly in
plastic wrap or foil. Then steam cook at 175°F until an internal
temperature of 160°F is reached.

✱ I sometimes stuff the pâté into sausage casings and
smoke it for about 30 minutes before I cook it, which gives it
a really rustic look and a wonderful flavor.

Sherried kidneys

I LOVE KIDNEYS—MY DAD ALWAYS BOUGHT PORK CHOPS WITH THE KIDNEY STILL ATTACHED. THIS IS A VERY EASY DISH THAT MATCHES THE NOBLE PIG'S KIDNEY WITH A LITTLE SHERRY OR MADEIRA. BE CAREFUL NOT TO OVERCOOK THE KIDNEYS OR THEY WILL BECOME DRY; IN FACT, LEAVING THEM A LITTLE PINK IS DELICIOUS.

Serves 4   Preparation time 15 minutes   Cooking time 20–25 minutes

2 tablespoons unsalted butter
1 onion, very finely chopped
2 teaspoons Dijon mustard
2 large pig's kidneys, skinned and cut into 3/4in pieces
1 tablespoon all-purpose flour
3/4 cup dry sherry or Madeira
3/4 cup any meat stock or gravy
salt and freshly ground black pepper
3 tablespoons chopped fresh flat-leaf parsley, to serve

✱ Heat the butter in a sauté pan until just foaming, then add the onion and cook for 3–4 minutes to soften slightly. Then add the mustard and cook for another 5 minutes.

✱ Add the kidneys and flour and mix well, then cook until the kidneys start to change color. Stir in the sherry or Madeira and stock or gravy and season with a little salt and pepper.

✱ Reduce the heat and gently simmer for 10 minutes; no more, or the kidneys will dry out too much. Adjust the seasoning and serve with lots of chopped parsley.

✱ This makes a nice appetizer, or a main course with steamed rice or even mashed potatoes.

Sautéed kidneys with green sauce

THE SECRET TO KIDNEYS IS TO AVOID OVERCOOKING THEM. ONCE GRILLED, BROILED, OR SAUTÉED UNTIL STILL PINK, LET STAND FOR 5–10 MINUTES AND THEY WILL BE PERFECT. THIS GREEN SAUCE IS MORE OF A PUNCHY, CHLOROPHYLL-PACKED SEASONING, WHICH COMPLEMENTS THE KIDNEY REALLY WELL. I SOMETIMES ADD A FEW ANCHOVY FILLETS OR EVEN A LITTLE FRESH GREEN CHILE TO THE OTHER INGREDIENTS FOR THE SAUCE, TO LIVEN IT UP EVEN FURTHER.

Serves 4   Preparation time 15 minutes   Cooking time 10 minutes at the most

$1/4$ cup olive oil
1 tablespoon unsalted butter
4 pig's kidneys, skinned and cut in half horizontally, but not completely through
2–3 tablespoons all-purpose flour
1lb thin asparagus spears, trimmed

SAUCE
$1/2$–$3/4$ cup extra virgin olive oil
2 fresh garlic cloves, peeled
2 tablespoons drained capers
salt and freshly ground black pepper
1 cup fresh basil
$1/2$ cup fresh flat-leaf parsley
$1^3/4$ cups fresh spinach

✱ Heat a large frying pan on the stove and add the olive oil and butter.

✱ Open the kidneys up and flatten so that you have a large double kidney but with the halves still attached to each other.

✱ Once the butter is foaming and changing color slightly, dust the kidneys in a little flour on both sides and add to the oil and butter. (Flouring not only gives a nice edge to the end dish but also reduces the amount of spitting from the pan.) Cook for 2–3 minutes, then turn over and cook for another 2–3 minutes; do not overcook. Remove from the pan and let rest.

✱ Add the asparagus to the pan and cook for a couple of minutes to take on a little color.

✱ Meanwhile, for the sauce, pour $1/2$ cup olive oil into a blender and add the garlic, capers, salt, and a little pepper. Blend until smooth, then add the herbs and spinach and blend again, adding the extra oil if needed to get a really thick green sauce. Spoon into a bowl and adjust the seasoning if necessary.

✱ Serve each kidney with a few asparagus spears and a good spoonful of the sauce—simple and delicious.

Simple kidney stew with baby apple dumplings

I LOVE DUMPLINGS IN ANY SHAPE OR FORM, AND I ESPECIALLY LIKE CRUNCHY-TOPPED ONES. HERE, TART COOKING APPLE, VERY FINELY CHOPPED OR GRATED, IS NEEDED TO CUT THE RICHNESS NOT ONLY OF THE KIDNEY BUT ALSO THE SUET, AND TO MAKE THE DUMPLINGS LIGHT AND FLUFFY. THIS IS A PERFECT WINTER APPETIZER FOR FOUR OR A HEFTY MAIN COURSE WITH MASHED POTATOES.

Serves 4   Preparation time 25 minutes   Cooking time 35 minutes

2 tablespoons olive oil
1 red onion, peeled and sliced into wedges
2 garlic cloves, crushed
12oz (2 medium) pig's kidneys, skinned and cut into $^3/_4$in pieces
1 tablespoon all-purpose flour
about 2 cups strong chicken or beef stock

DUMPLINGS
1 cup self-rising flour
$2^1/_2$oz suet (if unavailable, ask your butcher)
salt and freshly ground black pepper
1 very small tart cooking apple, such as a Macintosh,
    peeled, cored, and very finely chopped or grated
1 egg, beaten
about 2 tablespoons water

✱ Preheat the oven to 400°F.

✱ Heat the olive oil in a shallow ovenproof saucepan, roughly 12in in diameter; there is a reason for this that I will explain later. Add the onion and garlic and cook for 3–4 minutes so that the onion takes on a little color. Next, add the kidney and stir until it also takes on a little color.

✱ Add the flour and mix well, then add enough stock to cover the kidneys plus another $^1/_2$in. Bring to a boil and then turn off the heat.

✱ Now make the dumplings. Put the flour, suet, and salt and pepper into a bowl and mix well. Add the apple, beaten egg, and water and mix to a soft dough, the softer the better.

✱ Roll the dough into a thick sausage shape and cut into 16 small balls the size of a small walnut. Drop them into the hot kidney mix and place the whole pan in the oven. This is why I specified a shallow pan.

✱ Cook for 20–30 minutes, or until the tops of the dumplings are lightly browned and crisp. The bottoms will be beautifully soft and will have soaked up the lovely kidney stew. Serve with green beans or peas.

Braised hearts with 40 cloves of garlic & chicory

THIS IS A DECEPTIVELY EASY RECIPE, JUST RELYING ON TIME AND SOME FULL-FLAVORED INGREDIENTS. I BALANCE THE BITTERNESS OF THE CHICORY WITH A LITTLE SUGAR AND WHITE WINE. IT CAN BE COOKED IN A MEDIUM OVEN, BUT WILL SIMMER AWAY QUITE HAPPILY ON THE STOVE IN A PAN WITH A TIGHT-FITTING LID, ALTHOUGH YOU MAY HAVE TO ADD MORE BOILING WATER OCCASIONALLY. THE FINISHED DISH IS DELICIOUS AND HAS, BELIEVE IT OR NOT, A VERY MILD GARLIC FLAVOR.

Serves 4   Preparation time 20 minutes   Cooking time 2 hours 30 minutes

$\frac{1}{4}$ cup olive oil
4 pig's hearts, washed well and trimmed
2 large onions, roughly chopped
40 garlic cloves, peeled but left whole
2 heads of chicory, cut into $\frac{3}{4}$in pieces
1$\frac{1}{4}$ cups strong chicken or pork stock
about $\frac{1}{2}$ cup white wine
2 tablespoons sugar
salt and freshly ground black pepper

* Heat the olive oil in a saucepan.

* Cut the hearts into quarters lengthwise and then pat dry with paper towels or a clean kitchen towel.

* Place the heart pieces in the hot oil and brown well. Next, add the onions and garlic cloves and brown again over high heat. Add the chicory pieces and stir well.

* Add the stock, wine, sugar, and a good dose of salt and pepper to the pan, mixing really well.

* Bring to a boil, then reduce the heat, cover, and gently simmer for a couple of hours, or until very tender. Keep an eye on the pan, adding more boiling water if needed.

* Once cooked, check the seasoning and adjust if necessary. Serve with mashed potatoes and a little English or Dijon mustard.

Lightly braised liver with lettuce, peas, bacon & mint

I REMEMBER LIVER AND ONIONS AT SCHOOL IN THE OLD DAYS: DRY, STRONG, AND NOT VERY TASTY. MY GOOD FRIEND IS A DEVELOPMENT CHEF AT A MAJOR FROZEN MEAL PRODUCER, AND LIVER AND BACON BRAISE WITH GRAVY IS ONE OF THEIR BEST SELLERS ALL YEAR ROUND. MY MOTHER DID A GREAT VERSION AND HER SECRET WAS NOT TO OVERCOOK THE LIVER. SLIGHTLY PINK IS THE WAY TO GO WITH ALL LIVER IN MY VIEW. HERE IS A REALLY TASTY RECIPE THAT IS VERY EASY TO COOK AND LOOKS GREAT.

Serves 4   Preparation time 25 minutes   Cooking time 20 minutes

1 stick + 2 tablespoons unsalted butter
1lb 2oz fresh pig's liver, without tubes and skin,
   cut into 8 nice pieces on a slight angle, about 1in thick
salt and freshly ground black pepper
6–8 tablespoons all-purpose flour
3$\frac{1}{2}$oz smoked bacon, cut into very thin strips
1 small onion, finely chopped
$\frac{1}{2}$ head firm lettuce, such as Romaine or Iceberg, finely sliced
1 cup frozen peas
about 1$\frac{1}{4}$ cups chicken stock or 1$\frac{1}{4}$ cups boiling water
   and 1 chicken bouillon cube, crumbled
2–3 tablespoons chopped fresh mint
sugar, to taste

* Heat the butter in a large sauté pan large enough to seal all the liver at the same time.

* Dust the liver slices with salt and pepper and then flour them well.

* Once the butter is foaming, add the liver slices and cook for a couple of minutes to get a nice color. Turn over and do the same on the other side, leaving the liver still raw in the center. Remove the liver from the pan and set aside.

* Add the bacon to the pan and cook until the fat is released, then add the onion and cook for a few minutes, stirring well.

* Add the lettuce, frozen peas, and stock or water and bouillon cube and bring to a boil. Return the liver to the pan, turn down the heat to a simmer, and cook for a couple of minutes on each side; do not overcook. The stock will thicken from the flour on the liver.

* Add the mint and mix well, then re-season with salt, pepper, and sugar to taste. Serve immediately—the inside of the liver should be just pink.

Brain & avocado wrap

AS A YOUNG CHEF WE WOULD COOK LAMB'S AND PIG'S BRAINS ALL THE TIME—THEY WERE ALL THE RAGE IN THE 1970S. SOME YEARS AGO WHEN I VISITED FLORENCE WITH SOME GROCERY BUYERS, WE WENT TO A LOCAL RESTAURANT FOR LUNCH. THERE WERE NO MENUS, JUST A RATHER FLAMBOYANT CHEF WITH BRIGHT RED TROUSERS AND A FULL HANDLEBAR MOUSTACHE. THE FOOD ARRIVED IN WAVES, SOME GOOD AND SOME NOT SO GOOD. BUT THE THIRD COURSE WAS A LARGE FOIL PACKET THAT WAS SERVED IN THE MIDDLE OF THE TABLE. WE WERE GIVEN SMALL PLATES AND TEASPOONS. THE CHEF ARRIVED AND OPENED UP THE PACKET TO REVEAL A PERFECTLY INTACT, LIGHTLY STEAMED BRAIN. IT LOOKED LIKE SOMETHING FROM A HORROR MOVIE. IT HAD BEEN SEASONED WITH SALT, PEPPER, AND NUTMEG, AND WAS SWIMMING IN BUTTER. THE WAY TO EAT IT WAS WITH A TEASPOON, GENTLY SPOONING AWAY THE WOBBLY, DELICATE FLESH. IT WAS DELICIOUS, BUT I WILL NEVER FORGET THE LOOK OF REVULSION ON SOME OF MY FELLOW GUESTS' FACES. IN THE END THEY DID ALL TRY IT, HOWEVER. IN THIS VERSION I HAVE ADDED A FEW MORE TEXTURES AND FLAVORS, WHICH I THINK WORK REALLY WELL.

Serves 4   Preparation time 15 minutes, plus cooling/chilling   Cooking time 10 minutes

2 fresh pig's brains, washed well
1¼ cups cold water
2 tablespoons vinegar (any type will do)
salt and freshly ground black pepper
2 bay leaves
a few fresh parsley stalks
10 black peppercorns
¼ cup all-purpose flour, seasoned with salt and pepper
2 large eggs, beaten
6–8 tablespoons dried bread crumbs
¼ cup olive oil

WRAPS
4 x 10in soft flour wraps
¼ Iceberg lettuce, thinly sliced
4 thick-cut bacon slices,
    cooked until very crispy
2 hard-boiled eggs, peeled and halved
¼ cup mayonnaise
a few fresh cilantro leaves
1 avocado, peeled, pitted, and sliced into 8 thin slivers
2 scallions, finely sliced
1 carrot, peeled and finely grated (optional)

✱ Put the washed brains into a small saucepan and cover with the water. Add the vinegar, salt and pepper, bay leaves, parsley stalks, and peppercorns.

✱ Bring just to a boil, then turn the brains over, turn off the heat, and let cool completely. Chill well.

✱ Once chilled, remove the brains from the water and pat dry with paper towels. The brains will have set quite nicely, but not cooked through.

✱ Put the seasoned flour, beaten eggs, and bread crumbs into three separate dishes. Slice the brain into 8 small pieces and dip first into the seasoned flour, then the beaten egg, and finally the bread crumbs.

✱ Heat the olive oil in a sauté pan, add the bread crumbed brain pieces, and sauté for 2–3 minutes on each side; do not overcook. Remove from the pan and keep warm.

✱ Lay out a wrap on a cutting board. Place a little Iceberg lettuce down one end of the wrap. Top with a bacon slice, sprinkle with a little salt and pepper and add 2 pieces of bread-crumbed brain.

✱ Next, add half a boiled egg, a tablespoon of mayo, a few cilantro leaves, 2 slivers of avocado, and a sprinkling of scallions, plus carrot if you want. Fold the bottom edge over, then fold in both sides and finally roll up tightly. Repeat the process with the remaining wraps. Eat immediately.

Offal meatballs

I DEVELOPED THIS TAKE ON THE CLASSIC BRITISH DISH, "FAGGOTS," A LONG WHILE BACK AND IT STILL REMAINS ONE OF MY FAVORITES. MY CHEFS AND I IN THE KITCHEN BRIGADE WOULD MAKE THE DISH WITH GAME, INCLUDING A HARE VARIETY, AND THEY WOULD SELL REALLY WELL. I ADD HERBS AND GARLIC TO DEVELOP THE FLAVOR, AND REDUCING DOWN THE STOCK THEY ARE COOKED IN MAKES A REAL DIFFERENCE. OF COURSE, THE TRADITIONAL CRUSHED PEAS AND MASHED POTATOES ARE THE ONLY THINGS TO SERVE WITH THEM.

Serves 4   Preparation time 30 minutes   Cooking time about 1 hour in total

1lb 2oz pork belly
5^1/$_2$oz pig's liver, without tubes and skin
1 pig's heart, washed well
5^1/$_2$oz pork fatback
2 tablespoons vegetable oil
2 large onions, finely chopped
2 garlic cloves, crushed
^{1}/$_4$ teaspoon ground nutmeg
^{1}/$_4$ teaspoon ground mace
1 teaspoon dried sage
1 teaspoon dried thyme
^{1}/$_4$ cup chopped fresh flat-leaf parsley
2 eggs, beaten
6 tablespoons Worcestershire sauce
6–8 tablespoons dried bread crumbs
salt and freshly ground black pepper
about 3^1/$_2$ cups hot well-flavored brown pork or chicken stock

✱ Finely grind the meat, offal, and fat through a ^{1}/$_4$in plate into a large bowl.

✱ Heat the vegetable oil in a sauté pan, then add the onions and garlic and cook for 10 minutes to soften slightly. Add the spices and cook, stirring, for another 2 minutes, then let cool.

✱ Transfer the cooled onion and garlic mixture to a bowl, then add the ground meat mixture and mix well. Next, add all the herbs, the eggs, the Worcestershire sauce, and the bread crumbs, and season with salt and pepper.

✱ Mold the mixture into roughly 3^1/$_2$ oz balls, about the size of a small apple. Pack into a roasting pan nice and neatly and ladle in the boiling stock until it comes three-quarters of the way up the meatballs. Cover loosely with foil.

✱ Cook in the oven for about 30 minutes, then remove the foil and cook for another 20 minutes to reduce the liquid slightly. You can of course thicken the gravy with a little flour if you want to.

✱ Serve the meatballs with a little of the gravy, crushed peas, and mashed potatoes.

Mustard ear salad

I FIRST SERVED EARS ON MY MENU MANY YEARS AGO. IN FACT, AT THE TIME I OFFERED THEM FOR FREE TO GET GUESTS TO TRY THEM. THEY WERE A HIT AND BECAME A STAPLE ON THE MENU, COOKED IN MANY DIFFERENT WAYS. THIS WAS ONE OF THE MOST POPULAR.

Serves 4   Preparation time 15 minutes, plus cooling/chilling   Cooking time about 2 hours 15 minutes in total

2 large pig's ears
1 beef bouillon cube, crumbled
1 celery rib, sliced
1 carrot, peeled and sliced
1 onion, sliced
salt and freshly ground black pepper
3 teaspoons Dijon mustard
2 tablespoons chopped fresh basil
2 eggs, beaten
1 cup panko bread crumbs*

SALAD
1 large carrot, peeled
1/2 cucumber
1 small red onion, sliced
1/3 head crunchy lettuce, such as Iceberg, sliced
1/2 fennel bulb, sliced into slivers

DRESSING
1/3 cup extra virgin olive oil
2 tablespoons sherry vinegar
1/2 teaspoon Dijon mustard
1/4 teaspoon sugar
grated zest of 1 and juice of 1/2 lemon

✱ Remove any hairs from the ears by using a kitchen blowtorch or holding over a gas flame with tongs, then wash them well.

✱ Put the pig's ears into a large pan of boiling water with the bouillon cube, celery, carrot, and onion. Bring to a boil and season well, then reduce the heat and simmer very gently for about 2 hours until soft and tender. Add more water if necessary.

✱ Drain the ears and let cool, then pat dry. Chill the ears between two plates to help flatten them.

✱ Preheat the broiler.

✱ Place the ears on a cutting board and slice lengthwise into thick slices. Make a paste with the mustard and basil and then coat the ear slices with the paste.

✱ Put the beaten egg and bread crumbs into two separate dishes. Dip each ear slice into the beaten egg and then coat with the bread crumbs.

✱ Lay the slices on a sheet of foil in a roasting pan and broil for about 5 minutes on each side until crisp and pale golden.

✱ Meanwhile, prepare the salad and dressing. Use a vegetable peeler to slice the carrot and cucumber into thin, wide strips. Put into a large bowl and add the onion, lettuce, and fennel.

✱ Mix all the dressing ingredients together, then add to the salad ingredients and toss in the dressing.

✱ Place the salad on large plates, then arrange the warm, crisp ear strips on top.

*Panko bread crumbs are a Japanese version of bread crumbs made from crustless bread that is coarsely ground into larger flakes than regular bread crumbs. The result is lighter and crispier.

Blood sausage fritters and baby onions braised with balsamic

I LOVE BLOOD SAUSAGE IN ANY WAY, SHAPE, OR FORM, AND I HAVE ALWAYS COOKED WITH IT IN VARIOUS GUISES. I LIKE TO ADD A LITTLE TO A BRAISE OR STEW TO ADD AN EXTRA DIMENSION, OR TO A HOT POT. IT CAN WORK WELL TOO IN STUFFINGS AND SOME TERRINES, PROVIDING YOU ARE CAREFUL WITH THE AMOUNT YOU ADD. I ALSO USED TO PLACE A THIN SLIVER ON SOME TART APPLE PURÉE AND TOP WITH A FAT, JUICY ROASTED SCALLOP. HERE IT'S DEEP-FRIED AND SERVED WITH SOME BABY ONIONS BRAISED IN BALSAMIC VINEGAR TO BALANCE THE RICHNESS.

Serves 4   Preparation time 15 minutes   Cooking time 40 minutes

BABY ONIONS
3 tablespoons olive oil
1³/₄ tablespoons butter
2 tablespoons balsamic vinegar, plus 1 teaspoon to serve
1¹/₄lb baby (pickling) onions, peeled but root left on
sea salt and freshly ground black pepper
1 tablespoon snipped fresh tarragon

1 cup self-rising flour
pinch of salt
pinch of ground black pepper
1 heaping tablespoon chopped fresh flat-leaf parsley
about ²/₃ cup sparkling water or lager
vegetable oil, for frying
14oz piece of blood sausage (minimum weight), cut into ³/₄in round slices

✱ Preheat the oven to 400°F.

✱ First make the onions. Put the oil, butter, and balsamic vinegar into a deep baking dish. Add the whole onions (some can be halved if difficult to peel) and toss them in the oil mixture.

✱ Cook, uncovered, in the oven for 30–40 minutes until the onions are soft.

✱ Remove the dish from the oven, and while the onions are still warm, drizzle with the remaining teaspoon of balsamic and season with sea salt and ground black pepper. Mix the tarragon through lightly, tucking it into the onions.

✱ While the onions are finishing cooking, put the flour, seasoning, and parsley into a small bowl and beat in the sparkling water or lager until smooth, adjusting the amount of liquid to get a loose consistency.

✱ Heat about ³/₄in vegetable oil in a large, deep pan. Dip each piece of blood sausage into the batter and fry, in batches, in the hot oil for about 2 minutes on each side, turning once, until golden and crisp. Lift the fritters out with a slotted spoon and drain on paper towels.

✱ Serve the fritters hot with the braised baby onions and some fresh baby spinach leaves, simply dressed with lemon juice and cracked black pepper.

Pork rinds

OVER THE YEARS, I HAVE SOUGHT TO GET THE METHOD RIGHT NOT ONLY FOR HOMEMADE PORK RINDS BUT FOR CRACKLING. NOW I KNOW THEY ARE DIFFERENT, BUT WHAT I HAVE FOUND IS THAT THE BASIC PRINCIPLE IS THE SAME: TO EXTRACT AS MUCH FAT AS POSSIBLE FROM THE RIND SO THAT IT WILL CRISP UP PERFECTLY. IN THE FOLLOWING RECIPE I USE A DEHYDRATOR, BUT YOU CAN DRY THE SIMMERED RINDS ON A BAKING SHEET IN THE OVEN FOR THE SAME AMOUNT OF TIME. I DID TRY FRYING AND THEN BAKING THEM, BUT THE END RESULT WAS GREASY AND THE CRISPNESS WAS NOT EVEN CLOSE. SO WHAT YOU NEED TO DO FIRST IS TO CUT AWAY ALL THE INNER FAT FROM THE RINDS, LEAVING ¼IN AT THE MOST TO ENSURE A YIELDING, TASTY PORK RIND. A WORD OF WARNING: THE RINDS DO SPLATTER WHEN BAKING IN THE OVEN, SO LOOSELY COVER WITH FOIL OR BE PREPARED TO CLEAN YOUR OVEN, BUT IT'S A SMALL PRICE TO PAY.

Serves 4   Preparation time 10 minutes   Cooking time about 3 or 6 hours in total, but trust me it's worth it

1lb 10oz pork skin, with ¼in maximum depth of fat on the inside
⅔ cup vegetable or inexpensive olive oil, or melted lard
salt and freshly ground black pepper
malt vinegar, to serve (optional)

✱ Put the pork into a saucepan and add a little salt.

✱ Bring to a simmer and cook until when you pinch the rind (sufficiently cooled!) your fingernails will go through it easily. This should take about 35–40 minutes. I do this so that when the rinds are fully cooked you get an even bite, without breaking your teeth.

✱ Once the rinds are ready, drain well, place on paper towels, and dry thoroughly. Then either pop into a dehydrator set to 130–140°F and dry for 5 hours, or alternatively, place on a cake cooling rack set over a baking sheet and bake in the oven preheated to 275°F for a couple of hours. The rinds will then be firmer and ready to go.

✱ Turn the oven up, or preheat, to 425°F and spread the rinds out on a baking sheet. Liberally drizzle with the oil or melted lard and season well with salt and pepper. Cook for about 20 minutes until crispy and well blistered, turning over only when the popping sound has stopped coming from the oven; this way you will avoid burning yourself.

✱ Remove the sheet from the oven and drain the rinds well on paper towels—you will find that much of the oil and fat has cooked out.

✱ Dust with salt and pepper and serve warm; not too hot. Sprinkling with a little malt vinegar at the last moment is also delicious.

Smoked bacon & snout boulangère potatoes

I HATE WASTE AND HERE IS A GREAT RECIPE FOR USING UP EVERY PART OF THE BEAST. IT'S A REALLY NICE WAY OF ADDING GREAT TEXTURE AND TASTE TO A SIMPLE POTATO DISH, AND THE END RESULT IS VERY SATISFYING.

Serves 4–6   Preparation time 20 minutes, plus standing   Cooking time about 3 hours

8 pig's snouts, washed well
1 tablespoon salt
1/2 tablespoon ground black pepper
2 cups chicken stock or 2 cups water and 2 chicken bouillon cubes, crumbled
51/2oz smoked bacon or pancetta, chopped
4 large potatoes, peeled and sliced about 3/4in thick
2 large onions, finely sliced
2 garlic cloves, chopped
2 tablespoons chopped fresh flat-leaf parsley
1 tablespoon chopped fresh thyme
1 tablespoon chopped fresh sage
salt and freshly ground black pepper
1 stick + 21/2 tablespoons butter, melted, or 2/3 cup vegetable oil

✱ Put the snouts into a non-metallic bowl or dish, sprinkle with the 1 tablespoon salt and 1/2 tablespoon pepper, and let stand for a couple of hours in a cool place, or overnight in the fridge.

✱ When ready to cook, rinse well under cold water and put into a small saucepan. Cover with the stock or water and bouillon cubes and add the bacon or pancetta. Bring to a boil, then reduce the heat and simmer for 1 hour, or until the snouts are tender and very soft.

✱ Lift out the snouts with a slotted spoon and chop into small pieces. Measure the stock and make up to 3 cups.

✱ Preheat the oven to 425°F.

✱ Put the potatoes, onions, garlic, herbs, salt and pepper, and snouts into a bowl and really mix well. Pack into a 12 x 14in baking dish with sides 21/2in deep.

✱ Bring the stock and bacon or pancetta to a boil and then pour in the potato mixture. Press down well and cover with foil. Place on a baking sheet and bake for 1 hour, or until the potatoes are soft.

✱ Remove the pan from the oven and then remove the foil from the dish—the smell will be fabulous. Drizzle the melted butter or oil over the potatoes and gently press down with a potato masher.

✱ Return to the oven, uncovered, for about 15–20 minutes until the stock is reduced and the potatoes and snouts are nicely glazed.

✱ Remove from the oven, re-press, and serve as a main course on its own, or as an accompaniment to any pork dish.

Twice-cooked ears Chinese style with noodles

PIG'S EARS HAVE A LOVELY GELATINOUS TEXTURE AND FLAVOR THAT IS VERY HARD TO DESCRIBE. THEY WORK WELL IN ALL SORTS OF WAYS, SUCH AS IN STEWS, SALADS, SOUPS, AND EVEN SLIGHTLY SALTED AND CURED OVERNIGHT TO MAKE A LOVELY CONFIT. THEY ARE ALSO GREAT CRISPED UP IN THE OVEN WITH A SMEAR OF MUSTARD AND A CRUNCHY COATING OF BREAD CRUMBS (SEE PAGE 185), OR IN A STIR-FRY WITH LOTS OF VEGETABLES WITH A SHARP SAUCE, AND HERE I'VE GIVEN THEM THE FULL CHINESE TREATMENT. DO TRY THESE RECIPES—I'M SURE YOU WILL BE PLEASANTLY SURPRISED.

Serves 4   Preparation time 25 minutes, plus cooling/chilling   Cooking time 2 hours 15 minutes

2 large pig's ears
1 beef bouillon cube, crumbled
1 celery rib, sliced
1 carrot, peeled and sliced
1 onion, sliced
2 tablespoons hoisin sauce
2 tablespoons dark soy sauce
2 teaspoons sweet chili sauce
2 teaspoons rice wine vinegar
2 teaspoons honey
1 teaspoon Chinese five-spice powder
1 teaspoon cornstarch

NOODLES
1 1/4 cups small broccoli florets (including stems), sliced
salt
4 1/2 oz dried rice noodles
1 teaspoon sesame oil
1 tablespoon vegetable oil
2 cups shiitake or crimini mushrooms, sliced
1 garlic clove, chopped
2 scallions, sliced
8oz can sliced bamboo shoots or water chestnuts, drained
3 tablespoons oyster sauce
3 tablespoons light soy sauce
3 tablespoons water

✱ Remove any hairs from the pig's ears by using a kitchen blowtorch or holding over a gas flame with tongs, then wash them well.

✱ Put the ears into a large pan of boiling water with the bouillon cube, celery, carrot, and onion. Return to a boil, then reduce the heat and simmer very gently for about 2 hours until soft and tender. Add more water if necessary.

✱ Drain the ears and let cool, then pat dry.
Chill the ears between two plates to help flatten them.

✱ Preheat the oven to 375°F.

✱ Place the ears on a sheet of foil in a roasting pan. Mix the remaining ingredients for the ears to a smooth paste and use to coat the ears evenly.

✱ Roast the ears in the oven for about 15 minutes until nicely glazed. You may need to recoat with the juices a couple of times.

✱ Remove from the oven, place on a cutting board, and chop into large pieces.

✱ While the ears are roasting, add the broccoli to a pan of boiling salted water and cook for 2 minutes.

✱ Lift out of the pan with a slotted spoon and set aside. Pour the hot cooking water over the rice noodles in a bowl to cover and let stand for 3 minutes. Drain the noodles and then stir the sesame oil through them.

✱ Heat a large frying pan or wok and add the vegetable oil. When hot, add the mushrooms and stir-fry for 5 minutes. Add the garlic and scallions and stir-fry for 2 minutes, then stir in the drained bamboo shoots or water chestnuts, oyster sauce, soy sauce, and water.

✱ Finally, mix in the rice noodles and continue to cook for another couple of minutes until warmed through.

✱ Serve the noodles in deep bowls and top with the chunks of pig's ear; I sometimes mix the ears through the noodles.

Roasted stuffed pig's head with pistachios, dates & parsley ⟫⟫⟶

Roasted stuffed pig's head with pistachios, dates & parsley

WHEN I WAS A YOUNG CHEF WE USED WHOLE PIG'S HEADS ON BUFFETS ALL THE TIME. THEY WOULD BE ROASTED OR POACHED AND THEN STUFFED WITH ALL MANNER OF THINGS FROM TRUFFLES TO CURED MEATS AND FRUITS. THE CHRISTMAS BUFFET ALWAYS HAD A STUFFED HEAD COATED IN A SHINY BLACK GLAZE, THE EYES AND TUSKS DEPICTED WITH PIPED WHIPPED BUTTER—ALL VERY STRIKING. MY FATHER ALWAYS LOVED BRAWN, MADE FROM BOILING THE HEAD WITH TROTTERS, REMOVING THE MEAT AND SETTING IT IN THE FANTASTIC JELLY. THIS RECIPE IS DELICIOUS, AND THE CHANCES ARE THE BUTCHER MAY EVEN GIVE YOU THE PIG'S HEAD FOR FREE. GOOD LUCK!

Serves 8-10   Preparation time 40 minutes   Cooking time 2 hours 30-40 minutes, plus resting

1 boneless pig's head, in one piece (the butcher may make a small charge for boning the head)
3¼lb ground pork
2 onions, finely chopped
6 garlic cloves, crushed
2 eggs, beaten
2 heaping tablespoons roughly chopped fresh thyme
7oz Medjool dates (about 8 total), pitted and chopped
¾ cup shelled pistachios
grated zest and juice of 2 large limes
salt and freshly ground black pepper

GLAZE
½ cup honey
juice of 2 large lemons
pinch of salt

✱ Preheat the oven to 375°F.

✱ Open the head up and remove any scraps of fat or bloody parts.

✱ Mix the ground pork, onions, garlic, and eggs together well in a large bowl, then add the thyme, dates, pistachios, and lime zest and juice. Season well with salt and pepper and really mix well.

✱ Place the stuffing in the head cavity and gently roll up. This is the most important part. Using a trussing needle and strong string, start under the snout and carefully sew up the bottom and around the back of the head until you have sealed it well.

✱ Reshape the head so it roughly resembles a real head again. You can lightly pack around the head with foil to keep the shape, but I wouldn't bother too much.

✱ Place the head in a large roasting pan and season all over with salt and pepper. Using a large piece of foil, double or triple wrap the ears and the snout to keep them from burning. Roast in the oven for 2 hours.

✱ Remove the head from the oven—it will be nicely browned and looking good. Remove the foil from the ears and the snout. Mix the glaze ingredients together well, then use a pastry brush to brush all over the head.

✱ Return to the oven and roast for another 30-40 minutes, basting every 5-6 minutes until well browned.

✱ Once cooked, remove from the oven, loosely cover with foil, and let rest for 45 minutes. Then slice and enjoy—the lovely gelatinous meat and membranes, accompanied by the fruity stuffing, is worth all that effort and cooking.

Bitter chocolate blood & orange pot

I HAD A VERSION OF THIS MANY YEARS AGO IN A SMALL TOWN IN ITALY. IT WAS THE FINALE TO A STUNNING MEAL THAT BEGAN WITH A BOILED RABBIT SUBMERGED IN WARM, SAGE-FLAVORED EXTRA VIRGIN OLIVE OIL. THE LARGE BOWL WAS PASSED AROUND THE RESTAURANT FOR ALL THE DINERS TO HELP THEMSELVES. NEXT CAME A TINY PEASANT DISH OF BRAISED COCKSCOMBS, HEARTS, SWEETBREADS, SMALL VEGETABLES, AND VEAL TENDONS, ALL IN A SHARP, SLIGHTLY VINEGARY SAUCE—DELICIOUS. TO FINISH, WE WERE SERVED A DESSERT OF BITTER CHOCOLATE FLAVORED WITH EXTRA VIRGIN OLIVE OIL AND THICKENED WITH FRESH PIG'S BLOOD—WOW... HERE IS MY VERSION; I WILL LEAVE IT UP TO YOU TO REACH YOUR OWN VERDICT.

Serves 6-8   Preparation time 15 minutes, plus cooling/chilling   Cooking time 15 minutes

3 cups milk
7oz bitter chocolate (70 percent cocoa solids is perfect), broken up into small pieces
$^3/_4$ cup sugar
$^1/_4$ cup dried pig's blood (ask at your local pig farm or meat market)
$^1/_3$ teaspoon salt
$^1/_4$ cup extra virgin olive oil
finely grated zest of $^1/_2$ large orange

✻ Put the milk, chocolate, and sugar into a saucepan and gently warm, stirring all the time, until the chocolate is half melted.

✻ Add the pig's blood and salt and whisk well. Stir until the chocolate has fully melted and you have a nice shiny sauce.

✻ Bring just up to boiling point, then remove from the heat and let cool for 2 minutes. Stir well and then add the olive oil and orange zest. You may need to pass the mixture through a fine sieve, depending on the blood used.

✻ Pour into 6-8 small ramekins or glasses. Let cool completely, then chill well. Serve with a shortbread or other sweet cookie and a little lightly whipped heavy cream dusted with grated chocolate.

GLOSSARY

Air-dried
A generic term describing a product that has been cured and undergone a lengthy maturation period. How long this maturation takes depends on the thickness of the product, so the thinner it is the quicker it will be.

Bread rusk
A form of bread crumb commonly used to help bind and provide texture to a sausage. It will also soak up twice its weight in water. Melba toast is the US equivalent of bread rusk, or you can use bread crumbs as a substitute.

Brine
A solution of water and curing salt used primarily for curing bacon and ham.

Curing salt
Salt that has been blended with a curing agent. For salami production, for example, it often contains 0.6% sodium nitrite.

Deadweight
The term used to describe the carcass weight of any animal that has been slaughtered.

Dextrose
Commercial glucose, commonly used in the production of salamis.

Fat content
The amount of fat required to make a product. Within the trade, cuts of meat are bought according to how much visual lean meat (%vl) is needed.-

Fee (emulsifying agent)
Typically, e471, the mono and diglyceride fatty acid commonly used as an emulsifier and stabilizer in pâté-like products. Available from frutarom.com.

Hot smoked
A product that is cooked in a smoke-filled environment, typically at temperatures of between 168 and 185°F. Any kind of hardwood can be used for this process.

Lactic acid
One of the by-products of fermentation in a salami. Lactobacillus and pediococcus bacteria metabolize (feed on) the sugar content and produce lactic acid.

Natural casings
The small intestine of pigs, sheep, or cattle, which, cleaned and brined (salted), is used to make a whole host of products from chipolatas to salami.

Pave
Hog casing that has been dried and formed into sheets so it can be wrapped around products such as coppa and lomo.

pH Meter/pH

A device that accurately measures acidic and alkaline levels. A must-have for food safety if you are producing salami or any other fermented product.

Potassium nitrate

More commonly known as saltpeter, this is used as a curing agent in curing salt. Its use is strictly regulated and it is always best to source from reputable suppliers who will certify how much has been used.

Reddening

The term commonly used to describe the fermentation process in salamis. They start off a dismal gray color and after the starter cultures have worked their magic they turn a lovely red color.

Relative humidity

The ratio of partial pressure of water vapor in an air–water mixture to the saturated vapor pressure of water at a certain temperature. It's particularly relevant in the production of salamis and air-dried products.

Saltpeter

See Potassium nitrate.

Sodium ascorbate

The salt of ascorbic acid. Mostly used as a curing accelerator and antioxidant. It is typically used in all products that are made with curing salt.

Sodium nitrite

Used as a curing agent in curing salt, for example, in the production of salamis.

Sous vide

The French term for "under vacuum," it is a method of cooking whereby food is sealed in airtight bags and cooked in water at lower temperatures and for longer periods of time than in conventional cooking.

Starter culture

Bacteria such as lactobacillus that feed on sugars and produce lactic acid. Used in the fermentation process, it is responsible for giving salami its distinctive flavor and for lowering the pH value of the product.

Tempered

Frozen meat that has been placed in a fridge and allowed to soften.

Vacuum cooking

See Sous vide.

SUPPLIERS & USEFUL INFORMATION

Meat & ingredients

Heritage Pork International
Offers Berkshire certified pork, ham, bacon, and sausage. Naturally produced without nitrates or chemicals.
www.heritagepork.com
(712) 202-2357

Savory Spice Shop
Seasonings, curing salts, herbs and spices for sausages, hams, bacon, cooked and cured meats.
www.savoryspiceshop.com
(888) 677-3322

Smithfield
Sells ham, bacon, sausages, and other pork products online and at Smithfield retailers (see website for locations).
www.smithfieldmarketplace.com
www.smithfieldhams.com
(800) 926-8448)

William's Pork
British-style pork processor that sells British specialties like bangers and back bacon.
www.britishbacon.com
(910) 608-2226

Smoking & curing equipment

The Sausage Maker Inc.
www.sausagemaker.com

Cabela's
www.cabelas.com

Walton's
www.waltonsinc.com

Wood-burning ovens

Earthstone Ovens
www.earthstoneovens.com

Wildwood Wood Fired Ovens
www.wildwoodovens.com

Advice & support on keeping pigs

Canadian Pork Council
www.cpc-ccp.com

National Hog Farmer
www.nationalhogfarmer.com

National Pork Producers Council
www.nppc.org

USDA Economic Research Service
(Hogs and Pork)
www.ers.usda.gov

INDEX

INDEX

A book doesn't just happen, and there are a few people we would really like to thank.

Firstly Kyle, for giving us the opportunity to get nearly 60 years of work between us into written form. It was a lot of hard work all around, so thanks also to our fabulous KB team: editor Judith Hannam, who always has a smile on her face, copy editor Jo Richardson, editorial assistant Tara O'Sullivan, and designer Helen Bratby.

My now retired and very much missed agent, Mr. John Rush, and my not-retired-just-yet agent Luigi Bonomi. Thank you gentlemen.

The photographs are outstanding, so huge thanks to Peter Cassidy for all the hours laying in mud, pig poop, and even snow to get the right shots.

Thanks also to food stylist Mima Sinclair for some stunning looking dishes and Iris Bromet for styling.

My pig fascination started at a very early age with the late Mr. George King. He taught me that good meat comes from happy, well-fed, well looked after pigs, and that has never left me. Thanks to my baby brother Mike for all the graft in setting up and helping over the years. Later in life another person fired me up again—Peter Gott. His knowledge is second to none and he has always been at the end of the phone when I've needed help! John Rickatson, the affable man who breeds an amazing pig, thank you also. Please keep going! And to Mr. Paul Gutteridge, who helps me. I would struggle without him; he also doubles up as chief taster!

Finally Simon Boddy. He really is the man, and it's not often I say that. Phil Vickery

To Phil, a massive thank you for giving me the opportunity to help with this book. I have loved every minute. Also to Peter Cassidy and the team at Kyle Books for turning a shared passion into something truly wonderful. It was a pleasure to work with such incredibly clever and talented people—amazing! Simon Boddy

oink